# ◆ THE ASHTON SCHOLASTIC GUIDE

# Best Books For Children

## By Belle Alderman

## ASHTON SCHOLASTIC
SYDNEY AUCKLAND NEW YORK TORONTO LONDON

# Introduction

As an adult about to revel in children's books, you have a great treat in store for you. Children's books published since the 1960s rival their adult counterparts for innovative style, memorable characters, powerful storytelling and superb illustrations. Here is your opportunity as parents to explore this treasure trove, not only will you discover for yourself vast riches but your children will also reap the rewards.

It is important to remember that children are not born predisposed towards reading and books. You will have to encourage them by creating an environment rich with enticing books and promoting them with contagious enthusiasm. While there is no guarantee that such an environment will ensure your children become readers, there's no doubt you can demonstrate the pleasures and knowledge to be gained from reading. We all know children unable or reluctant to read, but these same children at one time opened books with the expectation of becoming competent, perhaps avid readers. Let's ensure that the books they do open in early childhood whet their appetites for more.

Experts on learning to read agree that the essentials for creating readers are:
- A wide range of interesting materials.
- Books which relate to what children know or want to know.
- An understanding, more experienced reader to act as a guide.

Sound simple? Here's where this book will help. *The Ashton Scholastic Guide To Best Books For Children* suggests many books to fulfil the first two requirements. Books of literary and artistic quality are included in the guide together with plenty of 'good reads' — books which may not survive the test of time but do entice readers. All you have to do is to match individual books to particular children.

It cannot be said too often that each child is unique and while each will pass through the same developmental stages, the rate of their development differs and appropriate literary experiences for them will also vary.

No list of recommended children's books could ever be complete given the some 40 000 currently in print with a further 10 000 published annually in the English language alone. The books listed in this guide are included as samples of the many excellent children's books available.

The books included in this guide have been carefully selected with the needs and interests of children from birth to early teens in mind. Here are the guidelines used in developing this collection:

- 'Good reads' of proven child appeal.
- Books of high artistic and literary quality.
- A range of the best books from Australia, America, Britain, Canada and New Zealand together with books translated into English and loved by children around the world.
- Authors and illustrators who are representative of the best in their type of writing and illustrating.
- A wide range of literary styles.
- Varied techniques of illustration, style and media.
- The best of the old and the new.

Most importantly, each book must have passed the essential test: Will it whet the appetite for more?

Happy reading!

Key

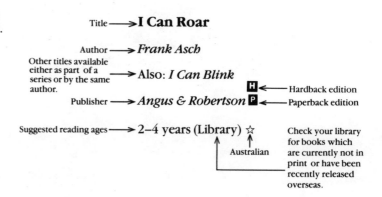

# Contents

# Creating life-long lovers of reading

### Start at birth!

Language experiences (including stories) should begin at birth. Babies can distinguish and respond to their caregiver's voice within a few days of birth. There is obvious power there in that human voice to comfort, amuse, stimulate and develop the child's emotional well-being and expanding intellect (eighty per cent of which is developed by the age of eight). Talk, chant, read, sing: offer any sort of language experiences that please baby and you. Not only does the communication create an important and special bond between child and adult, it also subtly links language, reading and books to a pleasurable experience.

### Establish a routine

As much for yourself as for your baby or child, set aside a special time for sharing books, ensuring a relaxing, pleasurable experience. Having a special time enhances the anticipation of an enjoyable activity and also demonstrates that reading holds high priority.

### Enlarge the purposes of print

Demonstrate to your pre-reading child, the power of language not only to give pleasure but to inform. Read aloud the signs on doors and buildings, labels on boxes, bottles, cartons and cans, words from shopping lists, video containers, greeting cards and letters and so on. In each case, emphasise print which relates to the child's immediate environment and interest. A sequence of squiggles (print), quite simply conveys a message. Thus begins the recognition that print has meaning.

### Read to relax and soothe, distract and transport

Reading is an inexpensive, transportable, easily operated form of entertainment, perfect for waiting rooms and queues, car trips, unfamiliar places and holidays. No environment is unsuitable and encores can be easily arranged.

### Expand story experiences

Relate books to a range of sensory experiences by encouraging your child to recall various sights, smells, sounds, tastes, and tactile features mentioned in a book when they encounter them in everyday life. Provide creative outlets for extending stories through art and craft, dramatisation, music, dance, puppets and flannelboard. Encourage children to create their own stories and preserve the best of these efforts. Books and stories are, after all, representations of life, so it is important to bring them within the child's understanding.

### Offer a range of story experiences

In addition to sharing books and telling stories at home, join storytelling and reading programs at your local public library. Some schools run reading programs as well. Shared experiences such as these, add another dimension to a story. Many children's books have been made into audio recordings, videos and cinema films. Rather than dousing enthusiasm, these alternate versions invariably create a demand for a story. Be prepared; capitalise on these versions by offering your children the books as well.

### Broaden reading preferences

We all have a tendency to want 'more of the same'. Introduce your child to as many different forms of literature as possible: poetry, folktales and fairytales, fables, myths, legends, epics, fantasies, science fiction, historical fiction, biographies, autobiographies, informational books–the range is endless. There's time enough to become the avid fantasy buff or 'facts only' reader.

### Keep abreast of children's books and their creators

With children in tow, browse, observe and discuss books in libraries, book stores and book fairs. Get to know librarians who specialise in children's books: their knowledge is vast. They know books and children and are eager to share their views. Find booksellers who have a serious commitment to children's books, who offer varied and comprehensive collections and have informed and enthusiastic staff. Take children along to sessions where children's authors and illustrators talk about their work. Short of a television or movie adaptation, nothing creates more interest in a book than meeting and talking to its creator.

### Demonstrate that books are important

Above all show your children that you consider books to be vital by letting them see you reading books. You are the most important and influential model in their lives.

## Keep reading in the forefront

Give books as gifts. Join children's bookclubs and browse through the selections in adult bookclubs for the popular children's titles. Subscribe to a children's magazine. Encourage children to develop a library of their own and to share their favourites with friends and with you.

## Read aloud

Recent studies of children's reading habits and interests reinforce the importance of reading aloud. Continue this activity even when children have become independent readers. The shared experience is pleasurable, but there are a number of other important reasons for reading aloud. Let's divide them into the advantages for the pre-reading child and to the child who can read independently.

The advantages of shared reading sessions for the pre-reading child are:

- They present the physical form of a book—it has a front, back, top, bottom and spine.
- They demonstrate the conventions of print—print has meaning, sequence, a direction on the page.
- They introduce literary forms and show how the conventions of these work.
- They develop an awareness of written language patterns as opposed to spoken language patterns.

And now to those advantages of reading aloud to the child who can read independently, although several of these apply equally to the pre-reading child:

- Reading aloud develops listening skills.
- It improves vocabulary, attention span and comprehension.
- It develops high expectations for print.
- It presents a variety of language experiences.
- It introduces books 'hard to get into'.
- It introduces classics which, although satisfying, are often difficult to read.
- It keeps the 'habit' of reading alive during periods when interest slackens.

- It builds an increasingly complex awareness of a wide range of experiences through literature.
- It provides a successful model to emulate.
- It demonstrates the value placed on reading.

In the final analysis, the most important reason of all for reading aloud is to demonstrate continually that books provide a wealth of interesting ideas.

# Nursery rhymes

Nursery rhymes have been handed down orally, some for hundreds of years, so their language is polished and memorable, just perfect for reciting to baby. Because so many suggest activities like bouncing, tickling, patting and clapping, they encourage interaction between you and baby and help to develop a close bond. As a bonus, nursery rhymes provide models of sound and language patterns, demonstrate that words have meaning and provide the first story experiences.

### Ride A Cock-Horse: Knee Jogging Rhymes, Patting Songs And Lullabies
*Compiled by Sarah Williams, illustrated by Ian Beck*
A vivacious and appealing collection of both familiar and unusual action rhymes which encourage rocking, jogging, patting, clapping, bouncing and dancing. The illustrations are sumptuous and yet have child appeal. This collection is sure to inspire much loving, cuddling and communicating. An ideal gift for new mum and baby.
*Oxford University Press* **P** 0–4 years

### Hector Protector And As I Went Over The Water
*Illustrated by Maurice Sendak*
These two brief nursery rhymes are given a totally new dimension by Sendak's expressive characterisation. Where rhymes often seem obscure the illustrator's talents can create new stories.
*Macmillan* **P** 3–5 years

### The Mother Goose Treasury
*Illustrated by Raymond Briggs*
The largest and most lavishly illustrated Mother Goose collection published. This oversized book has 408 rhymes and 897 illustrations. Colour and black-and-white illustrations alternate with some double pages having several rhymes to a page. Familiar and unfamiliar rhymes are included and the humorous illustrations feature both contemporary and traditional settings and dress.
*Puffin* **P** 0–6 years

### Drummer Hoff
*Adapted by Barbara Emberley, illustrated by Ed Emberley*
This delightful folk rhyme tells the story of the building of a cannon. Each of the brightly coloured soldiers, created in imaginative woodcuts, brings a part of the cannon. A surprise ending shows the cannon smothered in flowers and occupied by animals.
*Bodley Head* **H** 5–7 years (Library)

### This Little Puffin . . .
*Compiled by Elizabeth Matterson*
Designed for, and tested with, preschool children, this collection of songs, activities and rhymes is ideal to have on hand from birth. There are games to play with baby and a number of items feature subjects appealing to this age. There are brief helpful directions and an index of first lines.
*Puffin* **P** 0–4 years

### A Day Of Rhymes
*Selected and illustrated by Sarah Pooley*
These familiar nursery rhymes feature contemporary children in humorous, inventive illustrations. Sixty-one rhymes are accompanied by playful antics of multi-ethnic children in a variety of settings and warm interaction between loving adults and children.
*Bodley Head* **H** 0–4 years

### Rhymes Around The Day
*Selected by Pat Thompson, illustrated by Jan Ormerod*
A nursery rhyme collection in contemporary guise. A family with three children are illustrated in soft pastel watercolours in their daily activities but with the traditional rhymes. There is a sense of warmth and affection and the nursery rhymes are perfectly chosen to suit a contemporary family.
*Puffin* **P** 2–4 years

### Granfa' Grig Had A Pig And Other Rhymes Without Reason From Mother Goose
*Compiled and illustrated by Wallace Tripp*
Pigs, wolves, mice, foxes and dogs star in this Mother Goose collection of 121 verses. The choice features, though, are the numerous jokes in balloon dialogue and the comical illustrations. A good collection for those who especially enjoy humour and animals.
*Little* **H** 3–6 years (Library)

## This Little Pig Went To Market
*Nora Montgomerie, illustrated by Margery Gill*
An ideal collection of play rhymes for parents to use with babies. Included are numerous rhymes and songs such as: toe-and-finger counting, tickling, foot patting, rocking, leg wagging, face tapping, finger play, hand clapping, jig jogging and first singing games. One of the best and most comprehensive collections of this type.
*Bodley Head* 🄷 0–3 years

## Mother Goose: A Collection Of Nursery Rhymes
*Compiled and illustrated by Brian Wildsmith*
No child should miss Wildsmith's kaleidoscopic colours — lush, bold and exciting. Illustrations predominate in this collection of familiar favourites.
*Oxford University Press* 🄿 0–5 years

## Mother Goose Comes To Cable Street: Nursery Rhymes For Today
*Compiled by Rosemary Stones and Andrew Mann, illustrated by Dan Jones*
These twenty traditional nursery rhymes are set in street markets, playgrounds and docks, and have multi-ethnic characters, all of which give new perspectives to the old rhymes.
*Puffin* 🄿 4–7 years

## The Puffin Book Of Nursery Rhymes
*Iona and Peter Opie, illustrated by Pauline Baynes*
The Opies, lifelong researchers of oral literature, maintain many of us can recall up to 150 nursery rhymes. Here one can 'brush up' on two hundred forgotten ones. Indexing by subject and first line helps in finding favourites. For the curious, there are some notes on particular rhymes.
*Puffin* 🄿 2–5 years

## Tomie de Paola's Mother Goose
*Illustrated by Tomie de Paola*
Over two hundred rhymes are included, mostly drawn from the collections of folklore specialists, Iona and Peter Opie.
*Methuen* 🄷 0–6 years

## Oranges And Lemons
*Compiled by Karen King, illustrated by Ian Beck*
Twenty-two modern and traditional singing and dancing games are illustrated. Actions are both described and illustrated, and musical scores are included with suggestions for guitarists.
*Oxford University Press* 🄿 4+ years

## Quentin Blake's Nursery Rhyme Book
*Illustrated by Quentin Blake*
Featured here are sixteen unfamiliar nursery rhymes, all printed in large type and accompanied by Blake's whimsical illustrations.
*Collins Lion* 🄿 0–7 years

## Over The Moon: A Book Of Nursery Rhymes
*Illustrated by Charlotte Voake*
Here are 117 familiar nursery rhymes all illustrated with whimsical humour. Delicate watercolours alternate with sketchy line illustrations. This collection will appeal to those who like Victorian dress and a light, lively mood.
*Hodder & Stoughton* 🄷 0–6 years

## This Little Piggy
*William Stobbs*
William Stobbs specialises in illustrating single nursery rhymes in picture-book format. This one adds much to the story with two to three double-page extensions to the text and illustrations resembling a woven tapestry. Also: *Old Mother Goose And The Golden Egg; Pat-A-Cake, Pat-A-Cake; One, Two, Buckle My Shoe; Round And Round The Garden; A Frog He Would A-Wooing Go*
*Bodley Head* 🄷 0–2 years

### Marguerite de Angeli's Book Of Nursery And Mother Goose Rhymes

*Compiled and illustrated by Marguerite de Angeli*
For those who prefer traditional illustrations, this is a favourite. Many of the children and other people in the 260 illustrations are based on Marguerite de Angeli's own large family. A slight disadvantage is the number of rhymes per page; as not all of the 376 rhymes are illustrated there is some confusion in matching rhymes and illustrations.
*Doubleday* **P** 3–7 years
(Library)

### The House That Jack Built

*Rodney Peppé*
One of the most enduring and favourite childhood rhymes. Peppé provides illustrations clearly related to the story and introduces characters with humour and expression.
Also: *Simple Simon*
*Collins Lion* **P** 0–4 years
(Library)

### Ring O' Roses: A Nursery Rhyme Picture Book

*Illustrated by L Leslie Brooke*
Amusing and appealing illustrations of old favourites. Some poems such as 'Little Miss Muffet', 'This Little Pig Went To Market' and 'Humpty Dumpty' have several pages of illustrations which become extended stories.
*Frederick Warne* **H** 0–4 years
(Library)

### Mittens For Kittens And Other Rhymes About Cats

*Compiled by Lenore Blegvad, illustrated by Erik Blegvad*
Twenty-five traditional rhymes about cats are illustrated with great charm and detail in this small book.
Also: *This Little Pig-A-Wig: And Other Rhymes About Pigs; The Parrot In The Garret And Other Rhymes About Dwellings*
*Hamish Hamilton* **H** 3–5 years (Library)

### The Rebus Treasury

*Compiled by Jean Marzollo, illustrated by Carol Devine Carson*
These familiar nursery rhymes and songs are presented in a rebus format, where illustrations substitute for words. This encourages participation and helps in demonstrating that words stand for objects. The illustrations are either original, coloured pencil drawings or stamp art from nineteenth and twentieth century art.
*Methuen* **H** 3–6 years

### Chinese Mother Goose Rhymes

*Robert Wyndham (ed), illustrated by Ed Young*
Designed to be read vertically like a Chinese scroll, this is a collection of rhymes, riddles and games that Chinese mothers pass on to their children.
*Philomel* **H** 4–6 years
(Library)

### Humpty Dumpty And Other First Rhymes

*Illustrated by Betty Youngs*
Eight familiar nursery rhymes are included in this book, each with a double-page illustration of highly detailed embroidery and other woven fabrics.
*Bodley Head* **H** 1–3 years
(Library)

*Oranges And Lemons*

# Board books

**Board books are excellent for discussion and also for baby to enjoy independently. In most, babies or toddlers are featured in everyday experiences, others present a wide variety of appealing animals. The best have a brightly coloured, uncluttered appearance and are wordless, or have a bare minimum of text. It's a great joy to see baby recognise a familiar 'happening' in the slightly more advanced board books.**

### Max's Bedtime
*Rosemary Wells*
Max has trouble sleeping without his red elephant even though Ruby loans him all her animals. Finally Max is crowded out of the bed and discovers his red elephant under the bed. Great fun for children and parents alike. Bold colours, one to two simple sentences per page. Appealing expressions on these rabbits.
Also: *Max's Bath; Max's Breakfast; Max's Birthday; Max's Bedtime* (Max and Ruby Board Books)
*Collins* **H** 1–3 years

### Clap Hands
*Helen Oxenbury*
Four energetic and amusing toddlers busy themselves in typical pursuits such as clapping hands, dancing about, eating and banging pots and pans. The large boards are perfectly sized to illustrate individual personalities, while the spare text reflects the action and encourages interaction between adult and child.
Also: *All Fall Down; Say Goodnight* (Big Board Books)
*Macmillan* **H**
6 months–2 years

### The Park
*Eric Hill*
A teddy bear watches a pigeon eating, a butterfly attracted to flowers, a ball thrown in the air, a duck, a bear swinging, and a dog. Backgrounds are simple and objects simply outlined.
Also: *At Home; Up There; My Pets* (Baby Bear Books)
*Heinemann* **H** 1–2 years

### Good Morning
*Dick Bruna*
Bruna's boldly coloured, simply drawn books, whose characters' eyes always gaze intently at the reader, have great appeal. Simple identification of daily life activities: a bed, a child, bathing, eating, playing, friends and the house. On the last page, the little character waves goodbye.
Also: *Good Night*
*Methuen* **H** 0–3 years (Library)

### Mog And Me
*Judith Kerr*
Toddlers and older children all enjoy Mog, a lovable cat and family pet. Here Mog and a young child are shown sharing daily activities: stretching, washing, dressing, playing, eating and going to bed. The success lies in the familiar, simple, recognisable events.
Also: *Mog, The Forgetful Cat; Mog's Christmas; Mog And The Baby; Mog In The Dark*
*Collins Lion* **P** 1–3 years

### Animals In The Jungle
*Kenneth Lilly*
Well-detailed, coloured, highly textured photographic-style illustrations feature adult animals and their young. A few words identify the animals. Because of the animals' activities, these books have great appeal and are a good introduction to informational books.
Also: *Animals In The Country; Animals Of The Ocean; Animals At The Zoo*
*Methuen* **H** 3–5 years (Library)

### The Going To Bed Book
*Sandra Boynton*
An odd assortment of animals prepare for bed: have a bath, don pyjamas, brush teeth, exercise, then off to bed. The simple rhyming text winds slowly down as bedtime approaches. Plenty of sly humour in the illustrations.
Also: *But Not The Hippopotamus; Opposites; Moo, Baa, La La La*
*Methuen* **H** 0–2 years

## Holidays
*Helen Oxenbury*
Typical holidays at the beach with a toddler who pours a bucket of water on parents, has an ice-cream cone, covers bodies with sand, shelters from a wind. Softly shaded illustrations, sufficiently detailed with familiar objects. Good conversation starter.
Also: *Animals; Bedtime; Shopping; Helping* and an even simpler series: *Dressing; Working; Family; Playing; Friends*
*Walker* ⬛ 0–2 years

## My Daddy
*Mathew Price, illustrated by Jean Claverie*
A whimsical toddler asks simple questions such as, 'Who takes me to the swings' on one page and on the opposite page there is a flap with the activity and the answer beneath: 'Daddy'.
Also: *Smile Please!; Knock! Knock!*
*Five Mile Press* ⬛ 0–4 years

## Pets
*Valerie Greeley*
Intricately detailed double-page paintings feature animals in natural or other appropriate settings. Pets include the hamster, rabbits, tortoise, spaniel, cagebirds, tropical fish and cats. The paintings are highly realistic, and the settings are beautifully coloured with many attractive flowers.
Also: *Farm Animals; Field Animals; Zoo Animals*
*Blackie* ⬛ 1–3 years

## A Busy Day
*Chris Fairclough*
The best feature of this book is the colour photographs of a child's daily activities: riding a toy horse, snuggling in a lap, eating, crawling and playing. The infant frequently gazes at the viewer and is always cheerful and happy.
Also: *In The Park; Bathtime; Playtime*
*Hamish Hamilton* ⬛ 0–2 years

## Babies' Bodies
*Sally Kilroy*
Cartoon-style babies and toddlers feature, usually with a familiar object added for interest. Parts of the body are identified by a red arrow, and the appropriate word is included. A final illustration repeats the words and could be used as a guessing game. Lively and appealing, though eyes and noses are mere dots and dashes and there are others more realistic.
Also: *Animal Noises; Baby Colours; Noisy Homes*
*Viking Kestrel* ⬛ 1–3 years

## Where?
*Leo Lionni*
Simple, uncluttered collage illustrations feature two appealing mice in a series of activities. In *Where?* one mouse views the other: in a tree, in a shoe, in the grass, in a box, in a mousehole and in a bottle!
Also: *Who?; What?; When?*
*Pantheon* ⬛ 2–4 years

## Little Numbers
*Rodney Peppé*
Lots of toys familiar to children, such as bears, toy trucks, rabbits and dolls are shown brightly coloured on a white background. This series is uncluttered, simple and appealing.
Also: *Little Wheels; Little Dolls; Little Circus; Little Games*
*Methuen* ⬛ 0–3 years

*Mog And Me*

# For babies and toddlers

These small, square books, which resemble board books, concentrate on everyday experiences, here enhanced by a one or two sentence text per illustration. The best explore the baby's or toddler's relationship with family members within a loving, secure and familiar world.

## Here Comes John
*Bob Graham*
A familiar story of a snail and a crawling baby. Everything goes into baby's mouth but the snail is rescued just in time. Perfect for the very young child and the brief text encourages participation. Illustrations are sketchy, whimsical and amusing.
Also: *Here Comes Theo*
*Heinemann* 🄟 0–2 years ☆

## Reading
*Jan Ormerod*
Focus is on a father-baby relationship, a welcome view of family life. In *Reading,* and in a similar title *Sleeping,* father aims to read and sleep but a bored, adventurous baby interrupts these plans.
*Walker* 🄷 0–2 years

## The Blanket
*John Burningham*
When a well-loved security blanket cannot be found at bedtime, the entire household is turned upside down. Eventually, it turns up under the pillow. Simple sentences, small square format and themes within a child's experience make this and the others in the series toddler favourites.
Also: *The Dog; The Friend; The Cupboard; The Rabbit*
*Jonathan Cape* 🄷 1–4 years

## Cluck Baa
*John Burningham*
A toddler meets an array of animals and each makes a particular sound with the child joining in. Lots of fun in the pastel-coloured illustrations and plenty of activities and temptations to be noisy.
Also: *Skip Trip; Slam Bang; Sniff Shout; Wobble Pop; Jangle Twang* (First Words)
*Walker* 🄷 1–3 years

## 101 Things To Do With A Baby
*Jan Ormerod*
In multiple frames, here's life — good, bad, laughable and lovable — with baby. Mother, father and sister star as well as baby who eats, messes, and bathes with much love and affection and some natural jealousy.
*Puffin* 🄟 0–3 years

## My Toys
*Dick Bruna*
The familiar Bruna child features on the cover and toys follow: ball, bear, xylophone, crayons, top, train, drum, horn, blocks, beads, scissors, skipping-rope, whistle and puppets. The book can stand alone or be 'read' like a book. Familiar objects and wordless style encourage discussion.
Also: *Out And About; My Playtime; My Street; My Garden; My Animals*
Other series: *Miffy; Snuffy; Poppy Pig; Tilly And Tessa*
*Methuen* 🄷 1–3 years

## The Baby's Catalogue
*Janet and Allan Ahlberg*
Life with baby — mums, dads, brothers and sisters and all the myriad events in baby's life — is shown in this book. Babies and toddlers enjoy seeing themselves and their world. Arranged rather like a catalogue — groupings of food, clothes, garden utensils with the illustrations essentially as talking points.
*Puffin* 🄟 1–5 years

## Little Brown Bear's Playtime
*Claude Lebrun and Danièle Bour*
Little Brown Bear enjoys familiar childhood activities: resting and playing — with ball, boat, bucket and spade, rubber duck ring, green truck and blue car. Plenty of simple, clear, uncluttered and brightly coloured illustrations.
Also: *Little Brown Bear's Breakfast Egg; Little Brown Bear's Snowball*
*Methuen* 🄷 2–4 years (Library)

# Let's join in

Here are books which invite the reader and viewer to become part of the story. Mimicking sounds, feeling textured objects, looking for visual clues, viewing actions and guessing consequences, anticipating and predicting what is beneath a flap or behind a hole or what will happen with the pull of a tab or the turn of a page — these are only some of the activities encouraged.

## Dinner Time
*Jan Pienkowski*
In this exciting pop-up book, one animal is eaten by another until a shark finishes the tale. Each animal's mouth pops open with a turn of the page and in each instance a similar refrain is heard, ' "I'm going to eat you for my dinner." And he did'. Loads of appeal in an inevitable surprise coming up.
*Collins* **H** 0–5 years

## Henry's Busy Day
*Rod Campbell*
It's true: Henry never sits still! He is far too busy chewing slippers, scratching his back and so on. At the end of Henry's busy day he's fast asleep in his basket and his soft fluffy coat is there to stroke.
*Viking Kestrel* **H** 3–5 years

## Anno's Peekaboo
*Mitsumasa Anno*
The well-known game of peekaboo takes on new suspenseful anticipation with Anno's wordless simplicity. A pair of hands covers all but the top third of the page where various ears, heads and hats peep over, thus encouraging the viewer to guess what's beneath. The watercolours, set against large white spaces, add to an attractive format.
*Philomel* **H** 2–4 years

## I Can Roar
*Frank Asch*
A large circle cut-out on each page allows the reader's mouth and nose to become part of this book. A familiar animal appears with the circle cut out for the head and the sentence beneath states, 'I can . . . like a . . .' Parents and children will have great fun making the appropriate noises. Also: *I Can Blink*
*Angus & Robertson* **P** 2–4 years (Library) ☆

## Dear Zoo
*Rod Campbell*
A delightful flap book which is full of fun. A child asks the zoo for a pet, 'So they sent me a . . .' Under a flap is the animal and a rejoinder, 'He was too . . .' Children will enjoy guessing and the clues to the animal are in both the text beneath and the illustration. Finally a puppy is sent — and 'I kept him'.
*Puffin* **P** 2–5 years

## But Where Is The Green Parrot?
*Thomas and Wanda Zacharias*
A longstanding favourite which requires no reading, for the main objective is to find the green parrot hidden in the detailed illustrations. Many colours and objects to identify make this book great for discussion. Appealing scenes of toy chests, domestic interiors, a garden, a ship and the sky and a satisfying ending as the parrot returns home.
*Pan* **P** 2–4 years

## Who Sank The Boat?
*Pamela Allen*
A cow, a donkey, a sheep, a pig and a little tiny mouse pile into a boat for a row in the bay. One by one as they climb in the text asks, 'Do you know who sank the boat?' The rhyming language builds up the suspense and works with the animals' personalities and antics to create a humorous tale which children love.
*Nelson* **H** 2–7 years ☆

## Trouble In The Ark
*Gerald Rose*
Naturally, all the animals are feeling cooped up on Noah's Ark so when fly playfully buzzes the mouse, a noisy response follows. One animal after another makes various sounds, each illustrated to suggest the noise itself. At last a dove appears with an olive twig and Noah and his wife look forward to peace and quiet. But what should greet them on land — flies!
*Methuen* **P** 4–6 years

## Where's Spot?
*Eric Hill*
Spot, an inquisitive puppy, features in a successful series of flap books. When Spot's mother announces dinnertime she goes looking for her puppy. She asks, 'Is he behind the door?' and a flap reveals not Spot but another creature. The questions continue with surprises galore. Simple, boldly-coloured illustrations and large type feature.
*Puffin* **P** 0–5 years

## Do You Want To Be My Friend?
*Eric Carle*
The title introduces the adventures of a tiny mouse who greets the tail end of an animal on one page and the whole animal on the next. In a surprise ending, another mouse says 'Yes' then the head of a snake appears joined to its very long body which stretches from the first to the last page.
*Puffin* **P** 3 + years

## Gobble Growl Grunt
*Peter Spier*
Prepare your vocal chords for some vigorous exercise! Some six hundred animals parade across double-page spreads with their various sounds enticingly suggested. Humorous touches invite close inspection. A great communicative book!
*World's Work* **H** 0–5 years

## The Very Hungry Caterpillar
*Eric Carle*
A contemporary classic all children should meet. It is a story of a very hungry caterpillar which makes its way through a variety of food. The fun aspect is the hole eaten through the page. An unhealthy diet of sweets gives him a stomach ache! He finally spins a cocoon then emerges as a beautiful butterfly. A winner — colours, food, counting and science plus a very satisfying story.
*Puffin* **P** 3–6 years

## Peepo!
*Janet and Allan Ahlberg*
*Peepo!* is a book which your baby will enjoy for its rhythmic, soothing language. Slightly older toddlers will love the peepo game and the marvellously cluttered household and very important people: mother, father, grandmother and sister. In each case the peephole reveals a small portion of a scene and asks the viewer, 'What did he see?' The following pages reveal highly detailed family-orientated illustrations.
*Puffin* **P** 0–3 years

## Baby Talk
*Anne Miranda, illustrated by Dorothy Stott*
Soft and warm illustrations of a toddler and parents interacting accompany very familiar expressions. An added bonus are flaps which carry the small episode forward or enhance the brief comments. For 'no-no' there is a flap opening the bathroom cabinet door with toddler peering in. For 'big hug' the flap reveals parent and child doing just that. 'Bye-bye', 'all done' and 'peek-a-boo' offer more appealing events familiar to the very young.
*Dutton* **H** 1–3 years

*Trouble In The Ark*

# Alphabet books

When babies become interested in their surroundings, we adults naturally engage in 'point and say' activities to demonstrate the relationship between the real world and language. Alphabet and counting books with their splendid array of subjects are ideal for identifying, counting and discussing objects. These books may expand vocabulary and language experiences and encourage grouping and counting like and unlike objects. Their enticing illustrations offer a variety of artistic and social experiences and portrayals of different cultures and unknown worlds.

### Anno's Alphabet
*Mitsumasa Anno*
Alphabet books can be deceptively simple, such as this one. Plausible, yet impossible illustrations feature wood-grained objects attractive to the eye. Decorative borders also contain numerous objects beginning with the particular letter and for the puzzled there is a guide to some of these objects at the back of this wordless book.
*Bodley Head* **H** 3 + years

### B Is For Bear
*Dick Bruna*
A single small letter appears opposite an object in bold, bright colours outlined in black and beginning with that letter. A final page identifies all. Some challenging words include: igloo, eskimo, octopus and castle. Most can be matched with familiar available objects.
*Methuen* **H** 0–4 years (Library)

### Pigs From A To Z
*Arthur Geisert*
Large black-and-white sketches offer far more than a simple alphabet book. Seven hard-working little pigs briskly build an elaborate tree house. Each addition to the house highlights a specific letter of the alphabet which appears five times in different guises. Not all letters are easy to spot, nor are all the pigs. Therein lies the game-like aspect of the book.
*Houghton Mifflin* **H**
5–10 years

### The Moving Alphabet Book
*Tony King*
Small, coloured illustrations and photographs represent letters of the alphabet. Each page has two letters decorated with objects beginning with that letter. Opposite are two cut-out windows where, with a turn of an adjacent wheel, several objects appear, also beginning with the appropriate letter.
*Heinemann* **H** 2–4 years

### Bruno Munari's ABC
*Bruno Munari*
Munari is a master of simplicity and his rather unusual collection will expand the imagination. Several objects appear across double-page spreads which are artistic designs in themselves. Words and phrases highlight the letter shown. Some examples are: 'a dog and his dish outside a door' and a 'watermelon on a wagon with a wooden wheel'.
*Philomel* **H** 0–4 years (Library)

### A Peaceable Kingdom: The Shaker ABECEDARIUS
*Illustrated by Alice and Martin Provensen*
A rhymed verse with a difference. Each new line begins with successive letters of the alphabet, but following are several real and imaginative animals, four hundred in all. All are illustrated and the domestic detail of the Shaker culture is added for interest. The rhythm is catchy, and the unusual illustrations are on parchment-like paper. There is a note on the history of the Shaker movement.
*Puffin* **P** 4–7 years

### Animal Capers
*Kerry Argent*
An alphabetical parade of animals, including many familiar Australian ones, goes to the zoo. Each animal is resplendently coloured and engaged in some activity. The text consists solely of the animal's name in small and capital letters. A small bird appears in each scene engaged in humorous antics.
*Omnibus* **H** 2–5 years ☆

### A Is For Australia
*John Brennan*
Sharp, clear, coloured photographs set against bold black offer a truly all-Australian flavour — billies, cubbyhouses, dingoes, emus, milk bars, the Sydney Opera House, Uluru and Vegemite.
*Dent* **H** 3–5 years ☆

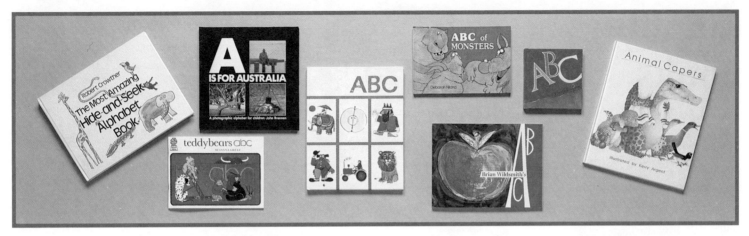

## ABC
*Elizabeth Cleaver*
The most attractive features of this book are the collage illustrations featuring torn paper, yarn and various objects which beg to be touched. Each letter on the left page is represented by three to ten objects artistically arranged on the page opposite.
*Oxford University Press* **H**
2–4 years

## The Most Amazing Hide And Seek Alphabet Book
*Robert Crowther*
This is a very successful toy book. By either lifting or pulling tabs, various animals and their names are revealed. The ingenious paper engineering often suggests the animal's movement — a woodpecker pecking at wood, a snake uncoiling. Each page features one to three letters in bold, black type, both small and large letters, set against a plain white background.
*Viking Kestrel* **H** 4–7 years

## Nutshell Library
*Maurice Sendak*
No child should miss the Nutshell Library, a diminutive set of four works. *Alligators All Around* is an alphabet book of alligators, featuring an active, rambunctious youngster. *One Was Johnny* is a counting book with a rhyming story about young Johnny, who threatened to eat ten creatures who promptly leave. *Chicken Soup With Rice* surveys the months of the year in rhyme. *Pierre* is a cautionary tale.
*Collins* **H** Set 4–6 years

## John Burningham's ABC
*John Burningham*
Capital and small letters and a word appear opposite brightly coloured, large illustrations of both familiar and unfamiliar objects. The appealing and humorous illustrations frequently feature animals and the unusual items include volcano, wasp and tractor.
*Jonathan Cape* **H** 0–4 years

## Jambo Means Hello: Swahili Alphabet Book
*Muriel Feelings*
Swahili is the most common African language and the twenty-four letters of this alphabet are presented here with a word for each letter. The book aims to briefly present aspects of the culture, so it is suitable for primary-aged children. The illustrations have a luminous, soft quality.
Also: *Moja Means One: Swahili Counting Book*
*Dial* **P** 6–10 years

## ABC
*Brian Wildsmith*
Objects are painted with bold colours and strokes and set against a solid coloured background. While most objects are familiar, there are a few unusual ones requiring some discussion, such as unicorn and windmill. For those who enjoy Wildsmith's artistic style, this is a winner.
*Oxford University Press* **P**
2–4 years

## Teddybears ABC
*Susanna Gretz*
The same lovable bears from *Teddybears 1 To 10* appear in a series of adventures such as flying, building and climbing. Most activities suggest the text with some clever jokes in the illustrations to enjoy. Interesting vocabulary includes 'gargling', 'idling', 'mucking about', 'quarrelling'. These bears never fail to appeal.
Also: *Teddybears 1 To 10*
*Collins Lion* **P** 3–5 years

## ABC Of Monsters
*Deborah Niland*
Monsters mean sure-fire attention. The ones here are lovable, rambunctious and, above all, engaged in comic pursuits. One is 'gobbling grandmas' (resisting), another is 'ogling ogres', and there's the one 'washing woollies' with a lamb being scrubbed in a tub.
*Hodder & Stoughton* **H**
3–5 years ☆

# Counting books

### 1, 2, 3 To The Zoo
*Eric Carle*
Open railway cars carry zoo animals beginning with one elephant, then two hippopotamuses, and so on up to ten. The illustrations are bold and brightly coloured collage. Below the large illustrations on the left-hand pages are small illustrations of railway cars showing, as each animal is added, the animals in boxes so eventually all animals are portrayed. A large fold-out page brings all the animals together in their new surroundings.
*Putnam* P 3–6 years

### One Woolly Wombat
*Kerry Argent and Rod Trinca*
An Australiana delight: from kangaroos and platypuses to magpies and kookaburras, the Australian animals abound in large, realistic and sophisticated illustrations. On the left-hand pages are rhythmic, rhyming couplets plus a single row of objects of the appropriate number at the bottom of the page. On the right-hand pages the realistic animals are given an imaginative touch.
Also: miniature edition and frieze available
*Puffin* P 4–6 years ☆

### One Panda: An Animal Counting Book
*Betty Youngs*
The artist has embroidered the animals in this counting book of numbers up to twelve. The illustrations are remarkable, textured and appealing. Koalas are included and a number of interesting animals such as camels, crocodiles, a moose, and a giraffe.
*Bodley Head* H 2–5 years (Library)

### 1 Hunter
*Pat Hutchins*
A hunter manages to miss all the jungle animals camouflaged in the background. As he passes each one, the next illustration reveals their presence. A guessing game, mystery, and beautifully stylised illustrations feature in this one-to-ten counting book. When all line up in the final pages, the hunter, amazed and frightened, runs for his life!
*Puffin* P 3–5 years

### Who's Counting?
*Nancy Tafuri*
Even the endpapers with their paw prints entice the viewer to follow a curious puppy's trail of adventure. Double-page spreads offer various flowers and animals in beautifully illustrated watercolours. There's the additional game of searching for the puppy amongst all the detail, plus the challenge of matching the number of objects with the large numerals and words.
*Greenwillow* H 3–5 years

### Over In The Meadow
*Illustrated by Ezra Jack Keats*
Collage and acrylic illustrations are very effective for this rhythmic counting rhyme which dates back to the 1800s. Familiar animals such as a turtle, fish and bluebirds are set in beautiful, natural surroundings. Great for chanting and singing.
*Scholastic* P 4–7 years

### Blue Gum Ark
*Jean Chapman, illustrated by Sue O'Loughlin*
An Australian adaptation of the traditional American counting rhyme, 'Old Noah He Once Had An Ark'. The full-page colour illustrations feature the whimsical antics of bunyips, possums, emus, echidnas and other bush creatures.
*Ashton Scholastic* P 3–7 years ☆

### How Many?
*Fiona Pragoff*
Here are clear colour photographs of familiar objects for counting one to twenty. Underneath the photographs are domino blocks with the matching number of black dots and the number. An artistically designed and wordless book which encourages discussion about colours, too.
Also: *Alphabet*
*Gollancz* H 3–5 years

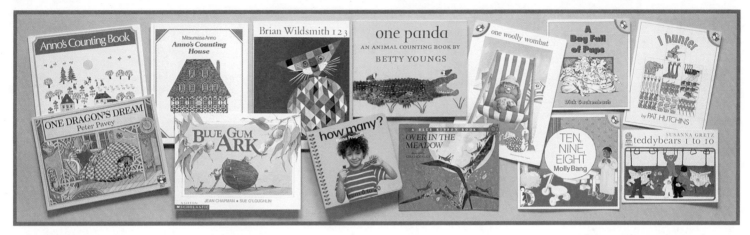

## One Dragon's Dream
*Peter Pavey*
Like most dreams, the dragon's features the improbable in a realistic guise. Teased, tried and sent to jail, the dragon eventually returns home. Each double-page spread is intricately detailed in lush, strong colours. Each number pictured has the same number — up to ten — of those objects in the illustrations. It's not always easy to find the objects, though. A counting book for those who enjoy visual games. Was it all a dream? Perhaps not!
*Puffin* **P** 5–10 years ☆

## Ten, Nine, Eight
*Molly Bang*
A brief, rhythmic text counts down from ten as a small girl prepares for bed. The text is lulling, gentle and the illustrations soft and warm. There's much love shown between father and daughter.
*Puffin* **P** 3–5 years

## Anno's Counting House
*Mitsumasa Anno*
Two houses on opposite pages and a group of ten children with various objects inside the house form the basics for the mathematical concepts of counting, matching, sorting, shapes and position.
*Bodley Head* **H** 4 + years

## Anno's Counting Book
*Mitsumasa Anno*
Beginning with an empty landscape, Anno adds objects, displaying at the same time, changing seasons, passing time and changing lifestyles. The numbers zero to twelve are illustrated.
*Macmillan* **P** 4 + years

## Teddybears 1 To 10
*Susanna Gretz*
These bears have charm and personality. From one to ten, they are seen as dirty and faded, then washed and dyed. In a grand gathering, all ten join together for a cup of tea.
Also: *Teddybears ABC*
*Collins Lion* **P** 3–5 years

## 1 2 3
*Brian Wildsmith*
There are so many levels here that it is a must for every child. Using circles, squares, rectangles and triangles, Wildsmith shows objects one to ten. These shapes are combined to form a house, a train, a body, an owl, a truck and so on. Then the viewer is asked to match a certain coloured, shaped object with an illustration. Colours are kaleidoscopic and brilliant and the effect is exciting.
*Oxford University Press* **P**
3–5 years

## A Bag Full Of Pups
*Dick Gackenbach*
A subtle counting book with a story sure to please pet-lovers. Mr Mullin must give away twelve puppies and each owner has a very different purpose in mind: from herding sheep to guiding blind people, riding a fire engine and going hunting. But the last new owner, a small boy, simply wants a friend.
*Puffin* **P** 3–6 years

*Blue Gum Ark*

# The world around me

These books stimulate the child's natural curiosity about their immediate and wider environments. Abstract ideas are made clear with familiar examples, clear, informative illustrations, appropriate vocabulary and a text that excites and challenges. Many are excellent stories as well.

### The Toy Shop
*Peter Spier*
Each of the four board books in this series is shaped like a building. Inside, simple sentences identify objects or events. In *The Toy Shop,* two children enter the amazing splendour of a huge toy shop and while selecting a gift for a friend, they examine everything. It is too detailed for babies, but toddlers will enjoy these books about objects of interest in their life.
Also: *My School; Food Market; Fire Station* (Peter Spier's Village Books)
*Collins* 🄷 2–4 years

### Airport
*Byron Barton*
Follows passengers arriving by car and bus to travel on aeroplanes. They check in, wait, the plane is prepared for take-off and a cut-away diagram of the plane shows various locations. The correct words are used so cockpit, stewardess, fuel and cargo hold are mentioned. Simple sentences explain each scene.
*Collins* 🄿 0–5 years

### Circles, Triangles And Squares
*Tana Hoban*
Stuning black-and-white photography wordlessly captures the shapes of circles, squares and triangles in the everyday sights seen in a city. Many include children thus adding to the interest. The viewer is encouraged to see the familiar in new ways.
Also: *Round And Round; Shapes And Things; Push–Pull, Empty–Full*
*Macmillan* 🄷 2–5 years

### My Day
*Rod Campbell*
A toddler invites the viewer to identify items in his world, such as: dress, home, garden, toys, shopping, park, countryside, zoo, teatime and bedtime. Each 'world' is presented in small frames with simple objects plus the accompanying word. No extraneous detail in these bright, colourful and familiar objects for children.
*Collins* 🄿 0–4 years

### Fast–Slow High–Low: A Book Of Opposites
*Peter Spier*
In typical Spier fashion, there's much to look at here. Over five hundred illustrations provide examples of opposites, such as high–low, smooth–rough, straight–crooked and hot–cold. Each concept is illustrated with a clear example, then several others follow. Loads of fun for all ages.
*World's Work* 🄷 4–7 years

### Animals Of Course! Mouths
*Jill Bailey*
Excellent quality colour photographs show a close-up with a balloon containing the question: 'Who has this mouth?' The next page reveals the full animal in its natural habitat.
Also: *Noses; Eyes; Feet*
*Heinemann* 🄷 2–4 years

### Numbers
*Jan Pienkowski*
Simple, easily recognised objects are illustrated in bold, bright colours. The numbers, words and objects appear opposite the pictures which place the objects in context, such as witches in the sky, ducks in a pond — one is half submerged! No space is left uncoloured and Pienkowski uses bright and compelling colours in unusual combinations. A very appealing book.
Also: *ABC; Colours; Faces*
*Puffin* 🄿 0–4 years

### Truck
*Donald Crews*
This wordless wonder follows a bright red truck through tunnels, over bridges, expressways and mazes of roads, through fog and rain, city and country. There is much to look at, including the various signs: trucking, tunnel, gas, speed limit, enter, exit; and much to discuss: traffic, air pollution, and so on.
*Bodley Head* 🄷 0–4 years (Library)

## Pink Pigs In Mud: A Colour Book
*Betty Youngs*
Ducks, donkeys, pigs, frogs, puppies, owls, chicks and parrots are featured in detailed illustrations. Each animal is a specific colour and the words opposite use a similarly framed phrase locating the animal 'in, on' etc. The final page of multicoloured objects asks, 'Which colours can you see in this picture?' Excellent for teaching colours.
*Bodley Head* 🄷 3–6 years

## Freight Train
*Donald Crews*
Excellent continuity as freight cars in different colours appear: red guard's van, orange petrol tanker, yellow grain hopper. Then the eight cars travel through tunnels, past cities, cross bridges, move in darkness and daylight. The train is slightly blurred to simulate movement and certainly achieves that effect.
Also: *Harbour; Light*
*Bodley Head* 🄷 0–5 years

## Animal Pictures
*William Stobbs*
Numerous animals are featured in their natural habitats. In each illustration something is happening, such as drinking water or catching prey. Some animals included are: leopards, antelope, a barn owl, field mice, ponies and butterflies.
*Bodley Head* 🄷 4 + years (Library)

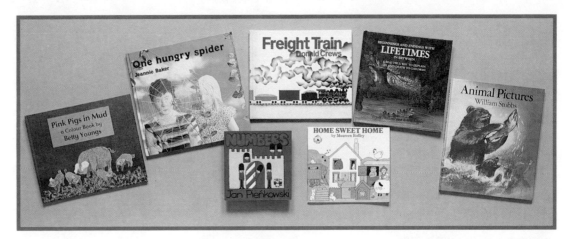

## Home Sweet Home
*Maureen Roffey*
The theme of this question-and-answer manipulative book is — who lives where? Similar sentence patterns, the elements of predictability, surprise and humour make this ideal for beginning readers. Stylised illustrations are appealing and the cut-aways and flaps are well-suited to the story. Children will enjoy guessing and correcting themselves, or 'being in the know'. Some of the cut-aways work both forward and in reverse, adding to the fun.
*Pan* 🄿 2–4 years

## Who Lives Here?
*Ron and Atie Van Der Meer*
Features a 'pull' tab. On the left-hand pages are four objects while on the opposite pages are enclosures. The viewer is asked, 'Who lives in the . . .?' A pull reveals which animal. Colours are not always realistic.
*Methuen* 🄷 2–4 years

## One Hungry Spider
*Jeannie Baker*
A two-page text at the back of the book gives detailed information on the spider here, Orb-web Eriophora. The illustrator calls her work 'relief collage' and uses actual materials, constructed to give the illusion of the real. Children will be attracted to this tactile, three-dimensional work and may be inspired to do their own.
*Ashton Scholastic* 🄿 5–8 years ☆

## Building A House
*Byron Barton*
A simple sentence identifies the tradesman and activity in each illustration which follows the step-by-step process of building a house. Bulldozers, hammers, saws and concrete-mixers are used by bricklayers, carpenters, plumbers, electricians and painters, and shown in clear, simple illustrations.
*Collins* 🄿 0–5 years

## Beginnings And Endings With Lifetimes In Between
*Bryan Mellonie, illustrated by Robert Ingpen*
Explaining concepts such as life and death to children is no easy task. This gentle, rhythmic text is a useful starting point. The illustrations add information and sustain the soft mood. The point is made that all things living — plants, people, birds, fish, trees, animals — live for a period of time then die.
*Hill of Content* 🄿 5 + years

## Whose Baby?
*Masayuki Yabuuchi*
Six baby animals are introduced successively with the line, 'Whose baby is it?' A turn of the page shows parents and baby together. Illustrations have photographic likenesses and poses show close family security. Animals such as the deer, fox, lion cub, seal pup and calf are shown.
*Bodley Head* 🄷 0–4 years

# First stories

A sprinkling of very simple stories should be included in your baby's or toddler's literary experiences. First stories are short, concentrate on a single character or one major idea, feature simple sentences, often with the appeal of repeated key words or phrases. Many also contain a liberal dose of humour. While the text remains simple, the illustrations often add amusing stories of their own. Sometimes the same character reappears in several stories and it's like meeting an old friend!

## Noisy
*Shirley Hughes*
In her inimitable, warm, cosy style, this author offers a toddler who joins in and listens to everyday noises: a telephone ringing, a baby crying, a plate breaking, pan lids clashing and a door slamming. The rhythmic, simple sentences wind down to a final illustration of all asleep. The ordinary life of a warm, secure family.
Also: *Bathwater's Hot; When We Went To The Park* (Nursery Collection)
*Walker* ⛁ 0–3 years

## Whose Mouse Are You?
*Robert Kraus, illustrated by Jose Aruego*
A warm story of belonging and family affection, but first an intrepid mouse must free his mother from the cat, his father from the trap and bring his sister home. The simple text is rhythmic and the rhyme breaks in just the right places to make the reader guess what happens next. An adventurous and satisfying tale.
*Puffin* ⧅ 2–5 years (Library)

## Animals Should Definitely Not Wear Clothing
*Judith Barrett*
A very funny book — everyone knows animals don't wear clothing, but here's what happens when they do. Snakes, porcupines, camels, hens and other animals appear in ludicrous situations. The text suggests why the animals should not wear clothing, but the illustrations convince.
*Atheneum* ⛁ 3–7 years

## Where Stars Grow
*Jan Blensdorf*
Wondrously appealing illustrations feature embroidery, padding, painting, beadwork and applique in this tale of a goat which admires the stars and seeks one for his own. A wise owl blindfolds the goat and leads him to experience sounds, tastes, textures and smells which could be those of stars. A surprise ending is beautifully constructed. While the text is not of equal quality to the illustrations, the sensory appeal and unique approach will hold great appeal for the very young.
*Oxford University Press* ⛁ 3–6 years ☆

## Bath Time For John
*Bob Graham*
Light-hearted and humorous family stories for toddlers and infants.
Also: *Where Is Sarah?*
*Methuen* ⧅ 1–3 years ☆

## Libby, Oscar And Me
*Bob Graham*
Emily is a master of disguise and in her various adventures is accompanied by her lovable pets, Libby the cat and Oscar the dog. All three have individual personalities revealed in very simple sentences and amusing illustrations.
*Collins* ⧅ 3–5 years ☆

## Little Blue And Little Yellow
*Leo Lionni*
Simple torn-paper collage represents little blue and little yellow and their varied coloured friends in this tale of friendship and family. When the two hug each other, they become green and are rejected by their families until they cry and once again become their original colours. Very satisfying reunion and a boon when talking about colours.
*Hodder & Stoughton* ⛁ 3–5 years

## My Book
*Ron Maris*
An ingenious flap book perfect for young children. A cat enters a gate, then a door, then goes inside the various rooms. A simple text states, 'My bathroom', 'My bedroom' and so on. The illustrations are amazingly detailed and full of familiar objects to talk about. Finally, the cat joins a child in bed and there, in a book being read, is just the scene in reality. Clever, secure feeling and a cosy 'goodnight' upon closing.
*Puffin* ⧅ 1–5 years

### The Chick And The Duckling
*Translated by Mirra Ginsburg, illustrated by Jose and Ariane Aruego*
Whatever the duckling does the chick does too, until the chick tries to go for a swim. The very simple sentences are similar and the chick always replies, 'Me too'. The surprise ending brings a smile.
*Puffin* **P** 2–4 years (Library)

### Rabbit's Morning
*Nancy Tafuri*
A warm story of families, adventure and home. A brief text states, 'The sun was hot' and a rabbit is pictured. Then the following double-page spreads illustrate what the rabbit sees: beaver, deer, frog, hummingbird and so on until finally arriving home to his own mother, father, brothers and sisters. Large illustrations encourage discussion. A final statement concludes: 'and rabbit came home'.
*Julia MacRae* **H** 3–5 years

### Rosie's Walk
*Pat Hutchins*
A modern classic tale of great charm and simplicity. Rosie the hen goes for a walk around the barnyard and all the while she is stalked by an accident-prone fox. With each page the fox is foiled in his attempts to trap Rosie. Stylistic and brightly coloured illustrations are used for this very funny story which young viewers enjoy as a private joke.
*Puffin* **P** 2–5 years

### Going Shopping
*Sarah Garland*
Mum, baby, little girl and dog are off to the grocery store. They pack into the car, drive down the road, get out of the car, go into the shop, walk down the aisles, pick up groceries and then drive home. Some interesting 'events' in the illustrations add a touch of appealing humour.
Also: *Doing The Washing; Having A Picnic*
*Bodley Head* **H** 0–4 years

### Sophie And Jack
*Judy Taylor, illustrated by Susan Gantner*
Here's an ideal story for the youngest with its elements of participation, humour and simple, natural language. Jack and Sophie are hippopotamuses playing a game of hide-and-seek while on a family picnic. Jack hides very successfully amongst some rocks, but the observant viewer will detect small ears and a tail. Colourful, whimsical watercolours.
*Corgi* **P** 1–3 years

### Sam Who Never Forgets
*Eve Rice*
Sam, the zookeeper, feeds the animals their favourite foods: leaves for the giraffe, bananas for the monkeys, red berries for the bear. But when elephant alone has not been fed, all the animals are sympathetic. Sam, in a satisfying conclusion, returns with a large wagon full of hay, for Sam never forgets!
*Puffin* **P** 3–6 years

### Have You Seen My Duckling?
*Nancy Tafuri*
Naughty duckling slips away and mother and her other seven ducklings go searching. A simple one-liner is repeated throughout as animals are met: 'Have you seen my duckling?' The secure feeling of reunion is comforting and children will enjoy repeating the question and observing the activities in the large, simple illustrations.
*Puffin* **P** 1–3 years

### Good–night, Owl!
*Pat Hutchins*
Poor owl! He can't sleep, various birds are keeping him awake, but his turn comes the night he wakes them all up! Each page has a repetitive text and introduces a different bird's sound, sure to encourage participation. The wonderful surprise ending may be anticipated but the pleasure is satisfying.
*Puffin* **P** 4–7 years

# Wordless books

These books your pre-reading child can 'read' to you! The illustrations alone create these stories with well-developed characters and often elaborately detailed action. Each story can have multiple interpretations, limited only by the imagination of the teller in tune with these inventive illustrators. More sophisticated wordless books appear in the category, Picture Books For Older Readers.

## The Ballooning Adventures Of Paddy Pork
*John S Goodall*
Any of Goodall's wordless adventure tales are enjoyable and especially those of Paddy Pork who features in several. Here, he travels in a balloon, lands on an island and saves a maiden in distress, survives a fierce storm, falls overboard, escapes from ferocious bears and arrives home, a hero. Half-pages make this tale one surprise after another and create a feeling of animation.
*Macmillan* **P**
3–5 years

## Changes, Changes
*Pat Hutchins*
An adventuresome couple build, according to their needs at the moment, various objects from blocks: house, boat, train, truck. The amazing aspect of the story is that exactly the same number, colour and shape of wooden blocks are used each time! A beautifully 'textured' feel to these wood-grain illustrations.
*Puffin* **P** 2–5 years (Library)

## The Train
*Witold Generowicz*
A book 5.3 metres long? Such a format is perfect for this merry chase scene. Two robbers are chased by two policemen across railway carriages and, as the chase proceeds, the pages fold out to reveal some unusual cargo and activities: bulls shoving cars off a platform, escaping monsters, an amazing milking machine. A book to enjoy again and again and again.
*Kestrel* **H** 4–7 years ☆

## Early Morning In The Barn
*Nancy Tafuri*
A rooster greets the day with his usual, 'Cock-a-doodle-doo' and then three little chicks leave their nest to investigate the barnyard and greet each animal. This excellent book encourages children to give the noisy response of each animal. The only text is the sound made by such animals as ducks, sheep, mice, turkey, goat, pig, horse and so on. Lots of clear and simple illustrations.
*Puffin* **P** 2–4 years

## Rain
*Peter Spier*
Rain, rain everywhere across double-page spreads and in numerous small framed illustrations. Brother and sister don rain gear and venture out to enjoy sights and sensations then return home to a warm bath and rainy-day activities.
Also: *Christmas!*
*Collins* **H** 4–7 years

## The Snowman
*Raymond Briggs*
A small boy lovingly builds a huge snowman who comes to life that night. The snowman is amazed by the human lifestyle, he starts at heat from the stove and likes dressing up and playing with toys but most of all he enjoys a rest in the freezer. Together the boy and the snowman fly away and eventually return home. The next day only a small melted snowman remains. A wonderfully warm story of adventure and friendship.
*Puffin* **P** 2–6 years

## The Trunk
*Brian Wildsmith*
Using brightly coloured collage and painted illustrations, Wildsmith shows a trunk with various animals racing to the top. In the final illustration, what the viewer presumes to be a tree trunk is revealed as an elephant's trunk.
*Oxford University Press* **P** 2–4 years

### Sunshine
*Jan Ormerod*
A gem of a story depicting the beginning of the day as a young girl wakes up, then rouses her parents. Father makes breakfast, then a last minute snooze and a mad dash to get ready in time. A warm caring family relationship here and father making breakfast is choice. Sunny colours to match the mood.
Also: *Moonlight*
*Puffin* **P** 2–5 years ☆

### Where Is Monkey?
*Dieter Schubert*
A little boy's stuffed pet seems forever lost but eventually turns up in an unexpected place. Beautifully detailed settings add appeal.
*Hutchinson* **P** 4–7 years

### Watch Me
*Pamela Allen*
A young boy on a tricycle jauntily shows off, balancing on the handlebars and increasingly doing more daring tricks. A frisky dog follows these antics. When the boy races downhill and tumbles on a stone, with subsequent sore knees, he is comforted by two little dogs.
*Nelson* **P** 3–5 years ☆

### Jack At Sea
*Philippe Dupasquier*
Jack lives in the era of British press-gangs in this tale of high adventure. When his friend becomes a victim and is taken aboard ship, Jack follows. Escape is impossible until the ship is wrecked at sea.
*Andersen* **H** 4–7 years

### The Gift
*John Prater*
Two children travel over traffic, down subways and below the ocean in an empty cardboard box. Watercolours feature in this multi-framed series of unforgettable surprises.
*Puffin* **P** 2–5 years

### Up And Up
*Shirley Hughes*
Shirley's ability to fly creates panic but allows some great adventures to take place. Here's a daring, adventuresome lass who achieves her greatest desire.
*Collins Lion* **P**
3–5 years

*Where Is Monkey?*

# First experiences

Many of life's experiences will be the first of their kind for the young child. These convincing stories are about such strong childhood emotions as jealousy over a new baby, fear of the night or the first day at playschool. Animals rather than children often feature, perhaps because such themes can be more sensitively handled by slightly removing them from the child's personal experiences.

## How Do I Eat It?

*Shigeo Watanabe, illustrated by Yasuo Ohtomo*
Here's a young bear with personality plus sure to attract children trying for independence like him. Cheerful and resourceful, nothing dampens his enthusiasm in various pursuits, despite his mistakes and misadventures. In this tale, little bear tries to drink soup, eat a piece of bread with a spoon and fork, pour strawberry jam, and ends up in a hopeless mess. But he then mixes it all together and eats it with his fingers. Success!
Also: *How Do I Put It On?; I Can Do It!; I Can Build A House!; Ready, Steady, Go*
*Puffin* **P** 3–5 years

## Peter's Chair

*Ezra Jack Keats*
Peter is upset when his parents paint his baby bed, high chair, and cradle pink for new baby sister, Susie. So he grabs his remaining blue chair and runs away. When he discovers he's too big to sit in the chair, he returns home and helps paint it pink. Collage artwork and simple illustrations add to this emotion-packed tale.
*Puffin* **P** 4–7 years

## Do Not Disturb

*Nancy Tafuri*
A family of five and their dog go camping in the forest. They blithely go about chopping wood, swimming, fishing, playing soccer, flying a kite and cooking dinner with little thought of the animals they are disturbing. A simple text and double-page illustrations invite the viewer to consider the relationship between humans and native wildlife.
*Greenwillow* **H** 4–6 years

## Feelings

*Aliki*
Exploring strong emotions is usually best done within the context of a story, but this book is the exception. Aliki uses a comic-strip layout mainly to present a wide range of small episodes in a child's life, all of which concentrate on an emotion such as anger or aggression. The humorous illustrations show how emotions are aroused and released. An excellent book for sharing between adult and child.
*Pan* **P** 5–8 years

## Leo The Late Bloomer

*Robert Kraus, illustrated by Jose Aruego*
For all the 'late bloomers', Leo's tale is very comforting. Leo, always watched by his father, couldn't read, write, draw, speak or eat neatly. His mother had faith that Leo was just a late bloomer. And one day he bloomed, and his first words were, 'I made it!'
*Puffin* **P** 3–6 years (Library)

## Dogger

*Shirley Hughes*
Dave dearly loves his stuffed pet, Dogger, so when one day he disappears, the whole family frantically search everywhere. The next day, Dogger turns up at a school fair, just bought by a little girl! Dave's kind sister swaps her newly won teddy for Dogger, and everyone is happy again.
*Collins Lion* **P** 4–6 years

## There's A Nightmare In My Cupboard

*Mercer Mayer*
What child has not imagined monsters in their cupboard at night? Armed with a popgun, a fearless boy decides to trap his nightmare but when he does, the nightmare begins to cry. The small boy tucks him into bed and snuggled together they both wait for the next nightmare to emerge! The nightmares look scary, but are lovable and comic at the same time.
*Puffin* **P** 4–6 years

### Alfie Gets In First
*Shirley Hughes*
A very satisfying tale of independence. Alfie, his mum and baby sister come home from shopping. Alfie races in, slams the door and locks himself in and the others out. On the right-hand page, Alfie is crying and on the left, outside, neighbours try different ways to get inside. Alfie, meanwhile, gets his chair and is thereby tall enough to open the door. Alfie is endearing and the illustrations give warmly detailed pictures of home life.
*Collins Lion* **P** 2–5 years

### Whistle For Willie
*Ezra Jack Keats*
What child has not tried to whistle and marvelled at the first successful one? Young Peter tries very hard and at last in a surprising moment whistles just when Willie his dog comes around. Collage and very simple illustrations suit this satisfying story.
*Puffin* **P** 3–6 years

### The Doorbell Rang
*Pat Hutchins*
What a painless, humorous story about sharing! Two children are all set to eat a plateful of biscuits when the doorbell rings and two further biscuit lovers arrive. Again and again the doorbell rings until finally there are twelve children and twelve biscuits. The doorbell rings again but this time it's Grandma with a plateful of biscuits.
*Puffin* **P** 3–6 years

### Harriet And The Roller Coaster
*Nancy Carlson*
George boasts to Harriet how brave he will be on the roller coaster. Harriet insists she's not scared to ride, but she doesn't sleep well that night. What a surprise when Harriet proves the braver of the two! Harriet is an appealing dog and has other adventures that feature emotions children will recognise.
*Puffin* **P** 4 + years

### Angry Arthur
*Hiawyn Oram, illustrated by Satoshi Kitamura*
Arthur gets very angry when his mother says it's time for bed, so angry that thunder, lightning, hailstorms, a hurricane, a typhoon, even a 'universequake' erupt! With every new furore, his family repeat, 'That's enough'. Eventually everything becomes just little bits in space and Arthur cannot even remember why he was angry!
*Puffin* **P** 7–10 years

### Felix And Alexander
*Terry Denton*
One day Alexander fails to return from his afternoon walk so Felix, his intrepid toy dog, bravely sets out to find him. Together the two conquer imaginative night monsters. Echoes of 'Hansel and Gretel' are here as Felix's stuffing leads the two friends home.
*Oxford University Press* **H**
4–7 years ☆

### It's Your Turn, Roger!
*Susanna Gretz*
It's Roger's turn to set the table and he rebels! He visits all the tenants in his building, sure that no one else must do such tasks, but he's repelled by mud pancakes, roots and snails. So he decides it's better to be part of a family and returns home and announces it's his turn to set the table.
*Collins* **P** 4–6 years

### The Tenth Good Thing About Barney
*Judith Viorst, illustrated by Erik Blegvad*
A child's first exposure to death is often that of a much loved pet and this tale is a very sensitive treatment of the theme. When Barney the cat dies, his youthful owner tries to think of ten good things about his pet. The tenth thing is very comforting and places death in a natural perspective. Gentle illustrations suit this small, warm book.
*Collins* **H** 5–7 years

### Umbrella

*Taro Yashima*

On her third birthday, Momo receives red boots and an umbrella and eagerly awaits rain. She imagines all sorts of reasons why she needs her umbrella, but her mother encourages her to be patient. Rain finally comes and the excitement is contagious. Not only is this the first time Momo has used her umbrella, but it is also the first time she has been for a walk without holding her parents' hands.
*Puffin* **P** 4–6 years

### My Brother Sean

*Petronella Breinburg*

Few books feature such expressive faces as Sean's on his first day at nursery school. Despite this much anticipated day, once there it's all tears until an understanding teacher, an array of toys and children to play with change his mood. The large close-ups of Sean crying create great empathy.
*Puffin* **P** 3–5 years

### Noisy Nora

*Rosemary Wells*

Nora's tale of wanting attention while baby Jack gets it all, is told in simple rhyme. She makes all sorts of noises and mother, father and sister repeat refrains such as, 'hush', 'quiet', and 'Nora! Why are you so dumb?' So Nora runs away and the family is upset, until she steps out of the cupboard with a 'monumental crash'.
*Collins Lion* **P** 3–5 years

### The Very Worst Monster

*Pat Hutchins*

Poor Hazel! She's completely ignored when her brother Billy, a new baby monster, is born. She tries everything but eventually decides she is the worst monster in the world with Billy the worst baby monster. This tale of jealousy, softened by an intriguing monster family, will be understood by many children with a new baby in their home.
*Puffin* **P** 3–6 years

### Timothy Goes To School

*Rosemary Wells*

The first day at school can be pretty traumatic when you're different. Timothy tries every day to be like the other children, but Claude makes sure each day is worse than the one before. And Claude is good at everything! One day Timothy meets Violet who feels just the same about Grace. In a happy ending, Timothy and Violet become fast friends.
*Collins Lion* **P** 4–6 years

### Tucking Mummy In

*Morag Loh, illustrated by Donna Rawlins*

All mothers (and their children) will relate to this story — here two young girls tell a story to mother who then falls fast asleep. They gently put her to bed. The simple text reflects the soft, warm feelings generated by the illustrations.
*Ashton Scholastic* **H** 5–7 years ☆

### What's Wrong With Bottoms?

*Jenny Hessell, illustrated by Mandy Nelson*

Raising the issue of sexual abuse is difficult but sensitive books shared between child and adult can help to allay concerns. A young boy, approached by his Uncle Henry, then explores his confused feelings with his understanding mother who provides supportive, informative comments. A particularly valuable aspect is the distinction between nudity, body functions and sexual abuse, all discussed naturally within a story format. The resolution is clear-cut and satisfying and the illustrations are attractive and helpful in dealing with the situation and emotions involved.
*Hutchinson* **H** 6–9 years ☆

### Pig Pig Goes Camping
*David McPhail*
Pig Pig's first experience of camping is a resounding success: he explores the woods; enjoys diving, fishing and boating; learns first aid, plaiting belts and cooking over a campfire. However, he proves too popular with the frog population and the camp director sends Pig Pig and his friends home. The illustrations all playfully reveal Pig Pig's ineptitude at camp life.
*Macmillan* **P** 4–7 years

### Good Night Ben
*Bernard Waber*
The first night sleeping away from home can be pretty scary, particularly if a teddy bear is a usual bed companion. When a scary ghost story is told, neither boy laughs as the other brings out his teddy. A comforting story of facing up to oneself and mastering feelings.
*Hodder & Stoughton* **P**
4–7 years

### Bedtime For Frances
*Russell Hoban, illustrated by Garth Williams*
Frances the badger cannot sleep, she is sure there are monsters and tigers in her room. Father always has a reassuring answer to Frances's fears but each time a new one emerges. A clever ending has Frances sound asleep. All the books in the series are whimsical, gentle and humorous stories about childhood emotions.
*Scholastic* **P** 4–6 years

### Benny Bakes A Cake
*Eve Rice*
Benny helps his mother sift, stir, ice and decorate his birthday cake. But Ralph, his dog, gets into the cake. Father saves the day with a wonderful new cake and there is a happy birthday after all. Warm family feeling and Benny and Ralph are sympathetic characters.
*Collins Lion* **P**
2–5 years (Library)

### The Red Woollen Blanket
*Bob Graham*
Many a blanket-loving child will relate to Julia whose devotion to her security symbol is revealed in an amusing tale. As Julia grows, her blanket shrinks as bits of the blanket are lost or destroyed. The climax arrives when Julia carts her tiny blanket to her first day of school and discovers she has finally outgrown it!
*Viking Kestrel* **H** 4–7 years ☆

### Happy Birthday, Sam
*Pat Hutchins*
Sam is sure that when his birthday arrives he will be much taller. But when it does, he still cannot reach his light switch, the clothes in his wardrobe, the front doorknob, until his grandfather sends him a small chair just right for standing on and reaching everything. A repetitive text and appealing illustrations.
*Puffin* **P** 4–7 years

### I Want My Potty
*Tony Ross*
'Yuuech,' says the princess, convinced that nappies must go. The queen proclaims, 'The potty is the place'. Humorous illustrations show the princess playing games with the potty, getting down to serious business and proudly displaying her efforts to a very embarrassed king. One day a small puddle demonstrates accidents sometimes happen. An appealing way to present an important topic.
*Andersen* **H** 1–3 years

### Jenny's Baby Brother
*Bob Smith, illustrated by Bob Graham*
Jenny is very unimpressed with her baby brother until the day he deliberately throws runny custard at her. From that moment on, Jenny discovers she has a little brother with personality plus. Humorous, warm illustrations perfectly suit this tale.
*Nelson* **P** 4–6 years ☆

# Picture story books

You're never too old to enjoy a good picture book and there are so many to share with your child. While the illustrations dazzle with their brilliant displays or attract with soft, subtle art, the authors offer every story imaginable — fantasy, adventure, mystery, daily life — often in exciting, innovative writing styles. Many of these stories have characters which reappear in new adventures. Stories which feature the elderly, disabled and various cultures are also included.

## Wombat Stew
*Marcia K Vaughan, illustrated by Pamela Lofts*
'One day, on the banks of a billabong, a very clever dingo caught a wombat . . .' So begins this amusing story of a dingo cooking his lunch. The bush animals conspire to save the wombat and teach the dingo a lesson. Lively illustrations showing animals with personality plus are a highlight of this book.
*Ashton Scholastic* **P**
4–8 years ☆

## William's Doll
*Charlotte Zolotow, illustrated by William Pene du Bois*
William wanted a doll, but his father gave him a basketball and train set instead. All his male friends called him, 'creepy' and 'sissy', but his grandmother understood and gave him one. To his father who complained, grandmother suggested William is practising being a father. A gentle, caring story that gives a non-stereotyped view of a boy.
*Harper & Row* **P** 4–8 years

## Max
*Rachel Isadora*
Max is a keen baseball player and plays every Saturday. Too early for the game, Max watches, then joins in, his sister's dancing class. He still plays baseball, but now 'warms up' for the game at dancing class. Pencil sketches are used for this clever story.
*Angus & Robertson* **H**
5–7 years

## Sebastian Lives In A Hat
*Thelma Catterwell, illustrated by Kerry Argent*
Sebastian is an orphaned baby wombat. A warm woollen hat is his new home and he is cared for by humans. Children enjoy his youthful concerns — a bottle, crawling and wobbling about, but most of all, a little pee. Illustrations feature a large, cuddly pink Sebastian in all sorts of contortions and activities.
*Omnibus* **H** 4–8 years ☆

## The Shopping Basket
*John Burningham*
This tale has it all — humour, repetition, challenge and adventure! Steven's mother sends him shopping but he's waylaid by various animals all of which he outsmarts. As he uses various shopping items they disappear from the illustrations, adding a counting aspect as well. This resourceful lad is to be admired!
*Puffin* **P** 4–6 years

## The Supermarket Mice
*Margaret Gordon*
Mice and cats usually don't mix, so this tale is an amusing switch. When the supermarket humans discover trails of mice around, they bring in Bounce, a rather overfed cat. But these resourceful mice befriend the cat by feeding him and he, in return, cleans up their trails. So all is happy once again. The mice's lifestyle is amusingly portrayed in small details. A surprising and satisfying ending.
*Puffin* **P** 3–6 years

## Watch Out For The Chicken Feet In Your Soup
*Tomie de Paola*
Joey is rather embarrassed by his Italian grandmother until his friend Eugene decides her ways are wonderful. Eugene loves her spaghetti and bread and her warm, loving ways, convincing Joey that his grandmother is tops all the way around.
*Prentice Hall* **P** 4–7 years

## Tin Lizzie And Little Nell
*David Cox*
Here's an Australian version of the familiar fable of the tortoise and the hare. The time is 1933 and William Winterbottom swears by his motor car, Tin Lizzie, while Billy Benson declares his mare, Little Nell, and sulky the best transport. Detailed portrait of country scenes, humorous escapades and a well-rounded text give great appeal.
*Collins* **P** 4–7 years ☆

### Swimmy
*Leo Lionni*
Swimmy, a tiny black fish, is the sole survivor of a school of red fish gobbled down by a large tuna fish. Resourceful and brave, Swimmy teaches a new school of red fish to swim together with himself as an eye. Now resembling a large fish, they chase big fish away. Collage illustrations are highly textured and imaginative.
*Knopf* **P** 3–6 years

### A Chair For My Mother
*Vera B Williams*
A warm family story which encourages repeated readings. After a fire destroys their possessions, Rosa, her mother and grandmother save their coins in a large jar. Their goal is a large, comfortable chair for mother to relax in after a hard day's work at the diner. Watercolour illustrations recall the patterns of the painter Matisse and have great sensory appeal.
*Julia MacRae* **H** 4–8 years

### There's A Hippopotamus On Our Roof Eating Cake
*Hazel Edwards, illustrated by Deborah Niland*
A young toddler invents an imaginative hippopotamus who can do everything she can't and can have what she wants! Illustrations feature a large, colourful, pink hippopotamus and an engaging youngster. Children with imaginative playmates will be doubly attracted to this book.
*Hodder & Stoughton* **H** 6–8 years ☆

### Dear Daddy . . .
*Philippe Dupasquier*
The bottom three-quarters of each page is devoted to Sophie's life at home while the top multiple frames reveal what her father is doing away at sea. Sophie's various letters to her father describing life at home make up the story. An innovative book.
*Puffin* **P** 7–10 years

### The Very First Lucy Goose Book
*Stephen Weatherill*
To the well-loved bears, rabbits, mice and pigs in children's literature, add Lucy Goose. In this series of five stories, she shows herself generous in spirit with a concern for others, a resourceful problem-solver, well-meaning hostess and inventive storyteller. Each tale is told in comic-book format with balloon dialogue.
*Pan* **P** 6–8 years

### The Tiger-Skin Rug
*Gerald Rose*
An old thin tiger envies the scenes of food, warmth and family comfort in the rajah's palace. In a clever ruse, the tiger becomes a tiger rug under their feet, but problems arise when he becomes less thin and moth-eaten and a bit smelly. His place is guaranteed when he heroically saves the rajah during a burglary.
*Puffin* **P** 4–6 years

### Where The Wild Things Are
*Maurice Sendak*
A contemporary classic tale of Max who creates mischief and is then sent to bed without his supper. Angered, Max imagines a land of wild things and himself as king. There he works out his anger and returns home to find his supper waiting for him. Superb, haunting illustrations accompanied by a poetic text have long-lasting appeal.
*Puffin* **P** 4–8 years

### The Three Robbers
*Tomi Ungerer*
Three robbers rob and plunder travellers on the road and one night take Tiffany, a little orphan girl, because she is the only treasure aboard the coach. In an unusual twist, the robbers turn good Samaritans, using their great riches to care for all the lost, unhappy and abandoned children they can find.
*Magnet* **P** 4–8 years

### The Robbery At The Diamond Dog Diner
*Eileen Christelow*
In this swift-paced adventure there are several clever and funny twists to the plot. Lola always wears her diamonds while she cooks in the diner until Glenda Feathers announces diamond robbers are in town. Hiding the jewels fails when a silly animal reveals the hideout and a kidnapping occurs. Clever Glenda foils the robbers' plan but a humorous ending shows even the best of ideas can backfire.
*Houghton Mifflin* **H** 6–9 years

### "Could Be Worse!"
*James Stevenson*
Grandpa invariably replies, 'Could be worse', to his grandchildren, Mary Ann and Louie's comments. In fact he seems to say and do much the same thing day after day, until he overhears his grandchildren comment that nothing interesting ever happens to him. Next morning he tells them a tale of high adventure. Here's an adventuresome and understanding grandfather and plenty of zany humour from this New Yorker magazine cartoonist.
Also: *The Great Big Especially Beautiful Easter Egg; Worse Than Willy!; We Can't Sleep; That Terrible Hallowe'en Night*
*Puffin* **P** 5–7 years

### Crunch The Crocodile
*Josephine Croser, illustrated by Carol McLean-Carr*
On the banks of a peaceful river lives a greedy crocodile who terrifies the other animals with his menacing refrain: 'My name is Crunch, And I want my lunch!' The full-page colour illustrations are amusing and highly detailed. Children love the animals' final victory over cowardly Crunch.
*Ashton Scholastic* **H** 4–7 years ☆

### Crusher Is Coming
*Bob Graham*
Because Crusher, the school football hero, is coming home to tea, Peter clears away his childish toys and prepares tougher entertainment. However, as the delightful illustrations reveal, Crusher prefers to play with baby sister Claire, and even wants to eat Mum's fairy cakes! An amusing and light-hearted story enhanced by whimsical illustrations.
*Lothian* **H** 4–8 years ☆

### Eyes
*Judith Worthy, illustrated by Béba Hall*
Beautiful full-colour illustrations of a variety of animals highlight their eyes. A light, amusing text gives details of each animal and will stimulate discussion. A book to share with very young children.
*Ashton Scholastic* **P** 3–5 years ☆

### Happy Birthday, Moon
*Frank Asch*
Bear thought it would be nice to give the moon a birthday present and travels to a tall mountain to chat. Bear discovers tomorrow is the moon's birthday and a hat is what is wanted. Little does Bear know that it's his own echo he has heard. In an amusing, believable scenario, the moon receives a hat and so does little Bear. Simple, enchanting illustrations have loads of appeal.
*Corgi* **P** 1–3 years

### Haunted House
*Jan Pienkowski*
One of the most inventive and successful pop-up books ever, both for its exacting, clever paper engineering and the popular topic of horror. While the child enjoys the rattling skeletons, fluttering bats and disappearing ghosts, the adult sharing will appreciate the send-up of all things horrific.
*Heinemann* **H** All ages

### Home In The Sky
*Jeannie Baker*
Set in New York, this simply told story is about a lost pigeon's return to its owner who lives on the roof of an apartment building. The illustrations, constructed of materials such as feathers, grass, bricks and mortar, and actual clothing, beg to be touched. Subway and city street scenes are amazingly true to life.
*Julia MacRae* **H** 5–8 years ☆

### Granpa
*John Burningham*
A close, affectionate relationship between a young girl and her grandfather is beautifully portrayed in their conversations, play and activities. One day Granpa is too ill to play. The next illustration simply shows a sad, wistful girl looking at Granpa's empty chair. The final illustration shows the young girl racing away with her baby pram. An excellent discussion book about death and the continuance of life.
*Puffin* **P** 7–10 years

### The Girl Who Loved Wild Horses
*Paul Goble*
A story of an Indian girl's wistful longing to run with the wild horses. The stylised illustrations in strong colours are outstanding. The text has a rhythmic quality and spare use of words which is excellent for reading aloud.
*Macmillan* **P** 5–8 years

*Crunch The Crocodile*

## The Farmyard Cat
*Christine Anello, illustrated by Sharon Thompson*
This is a delightful 'chase' story. The hungry farmyard cat is out to get the chickens, but she upsets the farmyard dog, bull, nanny-goat and horse. And who do you think wins 'the great farmyard chase'? The cat, of course.
*Ashton Scholastic* 🅿
4–7 years ☆

## First There Was Frances
*Bob Graham*
Here's a family story, warm and loving, but with a difference! Frances lives alone near the city but she is soon joined by Graham, Teak the dog, Marisol and Fraser the children, Grandma and a large assortment of goats, cats, guinea pigs, mice and a canary, each adding an amusing personality. But when the horses arrive, they move to the country! Illustrations add humorous additional stories.
*Collins Lion* 🅿 4–6 years ☆

## The Day The Teacher Went Bananas
*James Howe, illustrated by Lillian Hoban*
Few classes can boast of having a gorilla for a teacher, but this happens when Mr Quackerbottom, the new teacher, and a gorilla are sent to the wrong locations. The children learn some amusing lessons and find the gorilla a great friend. The sketchy, colourful illustrations add to the hilarity of the mix-up and demonstrate that even the absurd can seem real.
*Puffin* 🅿 5–8 years

*The Farmyard Cat*

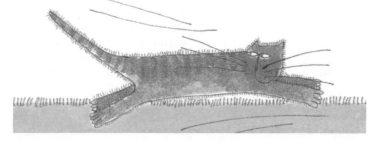

## Corduroy
*Don Freeman*
After a prospective buyer notices a missing button on his shoulder strap, Corduroy the teddy bear appears likely to remain on the department store shelf. Perturbed Corduroy searches for his button, braving a ride on the escalator and eventually claiming a button from a mattress. As new again, he is chosen after all and finds a friend. There's warm feeling in this story and Corduroy's most appealing thoughts about his environment and friendship have great charm.
Also: *A Pocket For Corduroy*
*Puffin* 🅿 3–5 years

## Whistle Up The Chimney
*Nan Hunt, illustrated by Craig Smith*
Mrs Millie Mack lives by herself and usually spends her winters knitting. But this winter a magical, bogey louvre door brings trains into her living room each time she burns a piece. Each illustration has marvellous detail of people and goods on the trains as well as Mrs Mack's living room. Great as a read-aloud and for poring over the illustrations.
*Collins* 🅿 4–7 years ☆

## Friends
*Helme Heine*
The theme of this whimsical tale is friendship between an unlikely trio of a rooster, a mouse and a pig. Together they share adventures, food (and tummy aches), decisions and avow eternal allegiance and togetherness. Watercolours of distinction and charm add humorous detail.
*Collins Lion* 🅿 0–5 years

## Mama Don't Allow: Starring Miles And The Swamp Band
*Thacher Hurd*
Miles receives a saxophone for his birthday but it's not long before his mother suggests he practises outside. There he meets up with other musicians to form the Swamp Band. But the townsfolk suggest they practise in the swamp. There their music is much appreciated by jovial dancing alligators. Unfortunately the Swamp Band is on the menu when the evening's over. This traditional song is presented in zestful, brightly coloured illustrations which exude music and dance. Musical score is included.
*Harper & Row* **P** 5–8 years

## The Polar Express
*Chris Van Allsburg*
A haunting, magical Christmas story with a message that warms the heart and ensures it will become a classic. A young boy travels on a train with other children and they all feast on sweets and hot chocolate and sing Christmas carols. The train's destination is the North Pole where, in a ceremony before hundreds of Santa's elves, the boy receives the first gift of Christmas — a magical bell from the reindeers' harness. Only those who 'believe' can hear the bell's ring. Throughout the boy's life, the bell sounds. Misty, richly coloured illustrations are as exceptional as the story.
*Andersen* **H** 5–9 years

## The Pearl
*Helme Heine*
Beaver is transfixed by a beautiful mussel shell, no doubt containing a valuable pearl. In a dream, he loses all his friends as they envy him the pearl and Beaver jealously guards his possession. Friendships and homes are destroyed before Beaver awakens and tosses his treasure away. A tale with a message, beautifully rendered in glowing watercolours.
*Puffin* **P** 5–7 years

Possum Magic

## Now One Foot, Now The Other
*Tomie de Paola*
Bobby is his grandfather Bob's namesake and they are very close. One day when Bobby is five years old, his grandfather has a stroke and is unable to talk or walk. Young Bobby then turns the tables by helping his grandfather learn to walk and talk again, much as he was helped as a youngster. Sensitively portrayed relationship and situation, and both characters have real personalities.
*Putnam* **P** 5–7 years

## Why The Chicken Crossed The Road
*David Macaulay*
Wild shenanigans and improbable catastrophes litter every page of this very funny story which answers the question posed. A chain of events sets off as a chicken startles cows, which stampede over a bridge, which collapses onto a train, which allows Desperate Dan the robber to escape. Just as all returns to normal, the cycle repeats itself.
*Houghton Mifflin* **H** 5–8 years

## Pinkerton, Behave!
*Steven Kellogg*
Pinkerton, an overly large, lovable dog, confuses all his owner's commands so he is enrolled in obedience school. There he causes havoc and is dismissed and sent home in shame. One night a burglar invades the house and Pinkerton's mixed-up commands make him a hero. The droll illustrations of the madcap obedience school and rowdy Pinkerton are great fun.
*Frederick Warne* **H** 5–8 years (Library)

## The Paper Crane
*Molly Bang*
Full colour, paper cut-outs add a three-dimensional quality to this American folktale. A restaurant owner's business begins to fail after a new highway re-routes traffic. But one day a mysterious stranger pays for his dinner with a paper crane which comes to life and dances. News spreads and people come from everywhere to see the magical bird. Though the bird eventually leaves, people continue to come to hear the unusual story.
*Morrow* **P** 5–9 years

## Round Trip
*Ann Jonas*
Stylised black-and-white illustrations have never been better than in this ingenious exercise in visual perception. A family makes a trip to the city, passing farms, trains, mountains to arrive, park the car, go to a movie and eat. Then, turning the book upside down takes the viewer home again. So clever are these illustrations that the eye is completely befuddled, momentarily. Should inspire similar efforts by children.
*Greenwillow* **P** 4–8 years

## Alexander And The Terrible, Horrible, No Good, Very Bad Day
*Judith Viorst, illustrated by Ray Cruz*
Nothing goes right for Alexander: ignored by his teacher, best friend lost, no dessert in lunchbox, on and on. Each scene is intricately sketched in fine black line. Everyone will recognise a tale like this! The comforting line is that 'some days are like that'.
*Angus & Robertson* **P**
6–8 years ☆

## Angelina Ballerina
*Katharine Holabird, illustrated by Helen Craig*
Angelina, a tiny mouse, thinks of nothing but becoming a ballerina. School, home and family all suffer until she is enrolled in Miss Lilly's ballet classes. After many long years, she becomes a famous ballerina. Much of the appeal is in the beautifully detailed illustrations of family life.
*Puffin* **P** 4 + years

## Meg And Mog
*Helen Nicoll, illustrated by Jan Pienkowski*
Witches, spells, cauldrons and airborne trips are some of the appealing subjects presented in bold colours and very simple text. Each of Meg, the witch, and her cat Mog's adventures have appeal and are great favourites. The hand-lettered text and simple illustrations will inspire budding artists.
Also: *Meg's Eggs; Meg At Sea; Meg On The Moon; Meg's Car; Meg's Castle; Meg And Mog Birthday Book; Meg's Veg*
*Puffin* **P** 3–6 years

## Avocado Baby
*John Burningham*
No one in the Hargraves family is very strong, except the baby who is fed on magical avocado pears. He can lift pianos, push cars and foil bullies and burglars. And he gets stronger every day!
*Collins Lion* **P** 3–6 years

## Rotten Ralph
*Jack Gantos, illustrated by Nicole Rubel*
Ralph, Sarah's pet cat, has a really rotten nature, but she loves him anyway. One day at the circus his despicable behavior is simply too much and the family leave him there. Poor Ralph is thoroughly mistreated, learns his lesson and is reunited with Sarah. Busy, inventive and very funny illustrations.
*Houghton Mifflin* **H** 5–9 years

## My Friend Jacob
*Lucille Clifton, illustrated by Thomas Di Grazia*
Sam is eight and Jacob is seventeen and they are best friends. Jacob, though mentally disabled, is able to teach Sam a lot and Sam tries to do the same for his friend. The story and soft pencil illustrations are sensitively done and show the difficulties and happiness of the disabled.
*Dutton* **H** 5–7 years

## Possum Magic
*Mem Fox, illustrated by Julie Vivas*
This Australian picture book best-seller continues to win hearts. Hush the possum is made invisible by Grandma Poss and only a trip around Australia restores her visibility. On the way, the two eat much-loved Australian food: Minties, pumpkin scones, Anzac biscuits, lamingtons, Vegemite sandwiches and much more. Text is beautifully crafted and the illustrations are endearing. A winner.
Also: *The Grandma Poss Cookbook*
*Omnibus* **P** 4–7 years ☆

## Bear Hunt
*Anthony Browne*
A simple but ingenious story. A white bear blithely outwits his aspiring hunters by drawing himself out of trouble. The jungle settings are full of visual incongruities and impossibilities.
*Scholastic* **P** 3–6 years

**33**

## Wilberforce Goes On A Picnic

*Margaret Gordon*

Just a simple picnic? That's what the text indicates, but the illustrations show Wilberforce the bear and his grandparents in numerous misadventures: a car breakdown, a rainstorm, Wilberforce doused in a pond, and much more. The humour lies in the detail in the illustrations and the contrasts between the text and illustrations.

*Puffin* **P** 3–5 years

## John Brown, Rose And The Midnight Cat

*Jenny Wagner, illustrated by Ron Brooks*

A contemporary classic tale of elderly Rose and her sheepdog, John Brown. When a mysterious black cat tries to join the family, John Brown rejects it totally until Rose takes to her bed. A story on many levels about jealousy, bargaining and even death. Illustrations, lovingly detailed, are a perfect complement.

*Puffin* **P** 4–8 years ☆

## Bossyboots

*David Cox*

Flash Fred, a fierce bushranger, meets his match in bossy Abigail who refuses to hand over her valuables when the mailcoach is under siege. Setting and costumes of early Australia add period authenticity and the fine line and watercolour illustrations have verve and humour.

*Collins* **P** 4–7 years ☆

## The Bunyip Of Berkeley's Creek

*Jenny Wagner, illustrated by Ron Brooks*

After a bunyip emerges from a creek, he sets out to find out who and what he is and is taken aback by a scientist who states simply, 'You don't exist'. Worried and unhappy, he stops at a billabong and there emerges another bunyip—so now both know who and what they are. A satisfying, philosophical tale about existence and self-identity.

*Puffin* **P** 5–8 years ☆

## John Patrick Norman McHennessy — The Boy Who Was Always Late

*John Burningham*

In this witty tale of a teacher who gets his comeuppance, the droll illustrations add to the cheeky humour. Young John is late for school because of three unusual encounters. 'Lies!' his teacher responds to his excuses, so when John finds his teacher pinned to the classroom ceiling by an enormous gorilla, he responds in similar fashion.

*Crown* **H** 7–10 years

## Bumble's Dream

*Bruce Treloar*

Mr Bumble collects junk with a purpose. He intends to build a flying machine, 'Bumble Bee'. Emily, his hen, and young Timothy, who advises and watches the proceedings, are left behind as Mr Bumble's dream comes true.

*Collins* **P** 6–8 years ☆

## A Cache Of Jewels And Other Collective Nouns

*Ruth Heller*

Children who relish new words will be delighted, not only with the rich collection of nouns but with the lush realistic illustrations of animals, plants and objects.

*Grosset & Dunlap* **H** 5–8 years

## A Lion In The Meadow

*Margaret Mahy, illustrated by Jenny Williams*

This completely new edition (original 1969) has a satisfying ending and illustrations which far surpass the first. A small boy insists there is a lion in the meadow, so a patient mother gives him a matchbox with a dragon in it to chase the lion away. But the dragon grows too big! The lion becomes a pet, living in the broom cupboard. Small children will empathise and the issue of what's real is left open to interpretation.

*Puffin* **P** 4–7 years

## The Kinder Hat

*Morag Loh, illustrated by Donna Rawlins*

Mummy agreed to wear whatever Jessie made in kinder class, but little did she expect to wear a fancily decorated ice-cream container on her head! Warm, supportive relationships between teacher and children, and parents and child. Illustrations offer a multicultural mix.

*Ashton Scholastic* **P** 3–5 years ☆

## Jesse Bear, What Will You Wear?

*Nancy White Carlstrom, illustrated by Bruce Degen*

Here's a warm family story of an endearing toddler bear's typical day. The rhythmic verse is rich and beautiful to read aloud while the illustrations are crammed with details of a child's familiar world. The text asks repeatedly, 'What will you wear?' and very inventive answers abound. For example, at night Jesse wears, 'Sleep in my eyes and stars in the skies, moon on my bed and dreams in my head'.

*Macmillan* **P** 3–5 years

## The Wild Washerwomen

*John Yeoman, illustrated by Quentin Blake*

There were once seven washerwomen who worked from dawn to dusk for mean Balthazar Tight. One day overwhelmed by yet another pile of dirty laundry, they rebel and create chaos in town. Seven woodcutters living in the woods dirty themselves horrendously, planning to frighten the wild washerwomen. The marvellous conclusion shows all living happily together and males and females alike doing everything. A humorous, subtle message on sex roles.

*Puffin* **P** 4–7 years

### Thirteen
*Remy Charlip and
Jerry Joyner*
Storytelling reaches an imaginative high standard in this series of thirteen stories spread across thirteen double-page spreads. The illustrations, in soft pastels, feature transformations, unfolding objects resembling animated films and other innovative techniques. A book which is visually sophisticated offering a new story upon each re-reading.
*Macmillan* **H** 5–10 years

### Digging to China
*Donna Rawlins*
Alexis wants to go to China to get a card for her friend's birthday so she decides to dig her way there through the earth. A charming story and the illustrations with their rich colours and intricate details of pagodas, cacti, flowers and lanterns are outstanding.
*Ashton Scholastic* **H**
5–7 years ☆

### Apt 3
*Ezra Jack Keats*
Two young boys seek the source of haunting harmonica music being played in their run-down apartment building. They discover a blind man who can play 'purples and greys and rain and smoke and the sounds of night'.
Collage illustrations effectively portray the mood of the story and the setting.
*Macmillan* **P** 6–10 years

### The Bionic Bunny Show
*Marc and
Laurene Krasny Brown*
Mild-mannered Wilbur is a rather ordinary bunny who is transformed into a television super-hero. The special effects, staging and costumes, which create a string of comical mis-adventures, are amusingly presented. A glossary of television terms appears at the end of the book, but television fans most likely know these and more.
*Collins* **P** 4–7 years

### How Tom Beat Captain Najork And His Hired Sportsmen
*Russell Hoban, illustrated by Quentin Blake*
Young Tom is particularly good at fooling around, a trait Aunt Fidget Wonkham-Strong finds most objectionable. She sends for Captain Najork to teach the youngster a lesson. But Tom's talent makes him the winner of such games as Womble, Muck and Sneedball. He even manages to hire a new aunt, Bundlejoy Cosy-Sweet. Highly inventive games and imaginative illustrations make this a delight.
Also: *A Near Thing For Captain Najork*
*Jonathan Cape* **P** 7–9 years

### D.W. All Wet
*Marc Brown*
Arthur is an appealing aardvark who appears in a number of holiday adventures and daily-life calamities such as losing a tooth, hating camp and detesting a new teacher. His little sister D.W. is brassy, cheeky and determined and often adds to the fun. Here D.W. is determined to hate the beach until Arthur tricks her into discovering its treats. Softly coloured illustrations and mischievous humour add a happy touch to this warm family tale.
Also: *Arthur's Nose; Arthur's Eyes; Arthur's Tooth; Arthur's Thanksgiving; Arthur's Halloween*
*Joy Street/Little* **H** 4–7 years

*Digging To China*

# Old favourites

Too often it's easy to ignore the old in favour of the new. These stories have survived for a good reason — children love them. Most are at least twenty-five years old and so may not look as flashy as newer titles, but try them. You'll find that the story has an inner truth which still speaks to children.

### The Story Of Ferdinand
*Munro Leaf, illustrated by Robert Lawson*
Ferdinand the bull is different from all other bulls. Instead of fighting, he enjoys simply sitting quietly and smelling flowers. But one day he is stung by a bee and his wild antics make him appear the perfect choice for the bullfights. What does Ferdinand do in the bullring? He smells flowers in the ladies' hair and quietly sits, refusing to fight.
*Puffin* **P** 4–7 years

### The Carrot Seed
*Ruth Krauss*
The faith of a small boy in his carrot seed sprouting defies all the family who repeatedly say, 'I'm afraid it won't come up'. But one day it does, 'just as the little boy had known it would'.
*Harper & Row* **P** 4–6 years

### The Little Engine That Could
*Retold by Watty Piper*
Many an adult can recite the refrain, 'I think I can — I think I can'. An engine, laden with toys and delectables for the children on the other side of the mountain, breaks down and many swanky engines refuse to help. Only a small blue engine agrees to help and, with perseverance, succeeds. The repetitive refrains capture the emotions.
*Collins* **H** 4–6 years

### Make Way For Ducklings
*Robert McCloskey*
This elderly title is proof that colour is not essential if the story succeeds. Mr and Mrs Mallard search for just the right spot to raise their family and finally find one in the public gardens of Boston, but not before they're rescued from traffic and amaze the city folk.
*Puffin* **P** 4–7 years

### Madeline
*Ludwig Bemelmans*
'In an old house in Paris that was covered in vines lived twelve little girls in two straight lines.' So begins the rhyming adventures of vivacious Madeline. In this tale she has an emergency appendectomy and later proudly shows her scar, becoming the envy of all the others. The rich architectural details of Paris add interest.
*Puffin* **P** 4–7 years

### The Runaway Bunny
*Margaret Wise Brown, illustrated by Clement Hurd*
One day a little bunny announces to his mother he is running away, but she replies, 'I will run after you. For you are my little bunny'. The little bunny suggests other ways he will get away, but his mother always says how she will bring him back. The text is repetitive, the language comfortable and there is a loving, secure ending.
*Harper & Row* **P** 3–6 years

### Harry The Dirty Dog
*Gene Zion, illustrated by Margaret Bloy Graham*
Harry hates baths with a vengeance and one day, with a bath imminent, he buries the scrubbing brush in the garden and runs away from home. How wonderful to get dirtier with each adventure but sometime later Harry becomes tired, hungry and misses home. But no one recognises Harry, now a black dog, when they are accustomed to a white dog with black spots! How Harry settles for a bath is as amusing as his further antics.
Also: *Harry By The Sea; No Roses For Harry; Harry And The Lady Next Door*
*Puffin* **P** 3–6 years

### Little Tim And The Brave Sea Captain
*Edward Ardizzone*
Little Tim fervently wishes to be a sailor but his parents say he is too young. So Little Tim runs away to sea and learns that a sailor's life is hard: scrubbing decks, repairing clothes, helping cook and battling ferocious storms. Little Tim eventually returns home, but he's soon off again in the other books in this popular series.
Also: *Tim All Alone; Tim In Danger; Tim And Lucy Go To Sea; Tim's Friend Towser; Tim And Ginger; Tim And Charlotte; Tim To The Lighthouse; Tim's Last Voyage; Tim To The Rescue*
*Puffin* **P** 5–8 years

### The Chicken Book
*Garth Williams*
Five little chickens each wish for a juicy morsel. The reader sees this very morsel just out of the chicken's sight. Finally mother hen suggests they must all scratch for their breakfast. A brief rhyming and repetitive text, plus the reader sharing in a secret, has made this an enduring tale.
*Collins Lion* **P** 3–5 years

### Blueberries For Sal
*Robert McCloskey*
On one side of the mountain, Little Sal and her mother pick blueberries for preserving. On the other side, Little Bear and his mother eat blueberries for their winter hibernation. Wandering from their mothers, both little ones mistakenly follow the wrong mother giving a big surprise to all. The funny mix-up has great appeal and the illustrations reveal the fiasco before the text.
*Puffin* **P** 5–7 years

### The Tale of Peter Rabbit
*Beatrix Potter*
Peter Rabbit's tale marks the beginning of the modern picture book where pictures and text are inseparable. No child should miss the challenging language and the delicate watercolours of Beatrix Potter. Peter's adventure in Mr McGregor's garden remains the favourite of Potter's animal tales, but the many others in charming, small formats hold great appeal, too.
*Frederick Warne* **P** 4–6 years

### Mike Mulligan And His Steam Shovel
*Virginia Lee Burton*
Mike Mulligan and his steam shovel, Mary Anne, could dig great canals, cut through mountains, lower hills and straighten curves. Eventually, Mary Anne is superseded by new equipment. The solution to this problem is ingenious and highly satisfying.
*Puffin* **P** 4–7 years

### Crow Boy
*Taro Yashima*
For six long years, a lonely Japanese boy attends school faithfully and because he does not join in activities, he is jeered by others. Then his special knowledge becomes clear in a very satisfying conclusion. A tale of being different and a loner has a strong message that is told with great sensitivity. A strong Japanese flavour to the illustrations.
*Puffin* **P** 6–9 years

### Good Night Moon
*Margaret Wise Brown, illustrated by Clement Hurd*
Goodnight stories, such as this one, survive for good reason. The text gently lulls both reader and listener into relaxing and the repetitive, short phrases put all the room's familiar occupants to sleep. Even the gradually darkened illustrations add to the bedtime mood.
*Scholastic* **P** 4–5 years

### The Story About Ping
*Marjorie Flack, illustrated by Kurt Wiese*
Little Ping the duck lives with his family on a boat on the Yangtze River. One night he is late returning and, knowing he will be spanked for being the last, hides in the grass along the bank. Ping almost becomes roast duck before he returns safely home, but he doesn't escape a spanking this time!
*Puffin* **P** 4–7 years

### The Story Of Babar, The Little Elephant
*Jean de Brunhoff*
The first in a long series of ever popular books about Babar. In this tale, we follow Babar from birth, witness his mother's death, life in the city, his education, return to the jungle, marriage to Celeste and his ascension to the throne. Stories are long and detailed but deal with strong emotions which maintain interest.
*Methuen* **P** 4–7 years

### Angus And The Ducks
*Marjorie Flack*

Angus is an inquisitive Scottish Terrier puppy. One day he breaks through a hedge to investigate the curious noises on the other side and discovers ducks. His very loud 'woof' startles them, but then they retaliate with hisses and nips. The language is simple but dramatic and the illustrations repeat the excitement.
Also: *Angus And The Cat*
*Puffin* 🅿 4–6 years (Library)

### Zozo
*Hans Rey*

Zozo, an African monkey, has a failing which keeps him in trouble — his insatiable curiosity. His misadventures are all those children would enjoy: trying to fly, dialling the telephone, and floating away with balloons. These episodic adventures are enhanced by the comic illustrations.
*Chatto & Windus* 🅗 3–6 years (Library)

### Little Toot
*Hardie Gramatky*

Little Toot's family are hard-working, respected tugboats, but he only wants to play. One day his antics cause the others to jeer and he decides to become worthy of his family, but not before he's swept out to sea and almost lost. The comic illustrations give life to Little Toot and break a very long picture-book text.
*World's Work* 🅗 4–7 years (Library)

### Millions Of Cats
*Wanda Gag*

A very old man and his wife wish for a cat to keep them company. The old man cannot resist bringing back 'hundreds of cats, thousands of cats, millions and billions and trillions of cats'. But because they cannot feed them all, the couple let the cats decide which is the prettiest, the one they will keep. Only a single scraggly cat is left after much argument and, with love and care, this one becomes a very beautiful cat. The refrain about the huge numbers of cats is a long-remembered favourite.
*Puffin* 🅿 4–7 years

### Anatole
*Eve Titus, illustrated by Paul Galdone*

Anatole, a French mouse and cheese connoisseur, is distressed that humans find him despicable and vows to change their opinion. Using his tasting skills, he leaves notes and directions for improving various cheeses in the Duval factory, with amazing results. The factory becomes famous and Anatole is daily given all the cheese he and his family can eat. There's a French flavour in setting, costumes and expressions.
*Puffin* 🅿 5–7 years (Library)

### Jeanne-Marie Counts Her Sheep
*Françoise*

Jeanne-Marie ponders how many sheep her pet, Patapon, will have and what she will eventually be able to buy with all the wool. Each page features some new item considered for purchase. Patapon always answers, 'But we shall stay in the green field where the daisies are white and the sun shines all day.' Simple illustrations have a child-like quality.
Also: *Springtime For Jeanne-Marie; Jeanne-Marie At The Fair; Noel For Jeanne-Marie*
*Brockhampton* 🅗 5–7 years (Library)

### Caps For Sale: A Tale Of A Pedlar, Some Monkeys And Their Monkey Business
*Esphyr Slobodkin*

A pedlar carries his caps for sale in an unusual way: one on top of the other and all sixteen of them on top of his head! After a long sleep under a tree, he discovers all his caps are gone and, above, sixteen monkeys are wearing them. None of his shouting retrieves his caps but a surprising event returns them all. A funny story with a repetitive text.
*Scholastic* 🅿 5–7 years

### The Happy Lion
*Louise Fatio, illustrated by Roger Duvoisin*

A happy lion once lived in a beautiful French town and was greeted every day by all the townsfolk. One day, when his door was left open, he went to visit everyone and was quite distressed to find them all running away in fear. Only a friendly boy responded to his overtures. The French setting and a few 'bonjours' add flavour.
*Bodley Head* 🅗 5–7 years (Library)

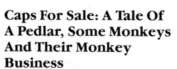

# Getting ready to read

These books have a double advantage. First and foremost, they are enjoyable stories, but they also have features which encourage the development of reading skills. The text is predictable with repeated words and phrases; a familiar sequence such as the days of the week or the seasons may feature; or a step-by-step process may be demonstrated; and rhythm and rhyme may be present too. These features encourage the development of reading skills such as predicting words, anticipating sentences, guessing meaning or maintaining the flow of the sentence.

Try some of these stories as your child is showing an interest in reading or when reading skills are developing. But don't forget, they're stories for enjoyment as well.

## The Big Sneeze
*Ruth Brown*
A humorous tale echoing the familiar story of the old woman who swallowed a fly. When a pesky fly lands on a dozing farmer's nose, one thing leads to another. A sneeze sends the fly into a spider's web. The spider captures the fly; the sparrow chases the spider; the cat pursues the sparrow and so on. Nothing is quite the same after this almighty sneeze!
*Beaver* **P** 3–5 years

## Old Macdonald Had A Farm
*Tracey Campbell Pearson*
Pearson has added to this familiar folksong, but all in keeping with the original. The illustrations reveal a loving and very busy family looking after many animals, each with an individual personality. A musical score is included.
*Collins Lion* **P**
3–6 years

## "Charlie Needs A Cloak"
*Tomie de Paola*
Charlie, a shepherd, desperately needs a new cloak, so from spring to winter he prepares one, first shearing the sheep, washing, carding, spinning and dying the wool, then weaving the yarn until finally — a new cloak. All the while, Charlie is kept company by a friendly sheep who makes the task more difficult, but these antics are shown only in the illustrations.
*Collins Lion* **P**
5–8 years (Library)

## Grandma Goes Shopping
*Ronda and David Armitage*
When Grandma goes shopping for food, she's easily distracted and purchases some rather unusual items, including an amiable alligator and a variegated vicuna. Each new acquisition is repeated in the text and illustrations. This tale is a pleasure to view and read aloud.
*Puffin* **P** 3–6 years

## Wilfrid Gordon McDonald Partridge
*Mem Fox, illustrated by Julie Vivas*
Youthful Wilfrid befriends elderly Nancy next door and solves a perplexing problem in a touching, convincing manner. One after the other he offers gifts from his world that conjure up her lost memories. Watercolour illustrations are light and delicate, matching the story's mood.
*Puffin* **P** 4–8 years ☆

## King Bidgood's In The Bathtub
*Audrey Wood, illustrated by Don Wood*
A fun-loving king refuses to emerge from his bathtub to rule his kingdom. Various members of the court try to tempt his lordship out but each one ends up in the bathtub too. Wondrous details of a Renaissance court delight the eye.
*Harcourt, Brace Jovanovich* **H**
4–6 years

### Mig The Pig
*Colin and Jacqui Hawkins*
Mig the pig is engaged in rather silly doings, all rhyming with pig. Two small caterpillars meanwhile make absurd comments. Good fun with sounds, rhymes and comic illustrations.
Also: *Jen The Hen*
*Puffin* 🅿 4 + years

### Bunny Rabbit Rebus: A Story In Words And Pictures
*David A Adler, illustrated by Madelaine Gill Linden*
Here small pictures and letters substitute for missing words and the reader is led through the story of a mother rabbit trying to find food for her son. He's rather greedy and keeping up with his appetite is most difficult. All the while mother rabbit gathers food, her son is busy eating, so in a humorous ending mother rabbit enjoys the lettuce and carrots herself.
*Puffin* 🅿 5–8 years

### Aardvark's Picnic
*Jon Atlas Higham*
Aardvark has invited all his friends to a picnic with ants on the menu. But all the ants have disappeared and Aardvark seeks help from the jungle animals. The monkey, crocodile, toad, snake and elephant all suggest their favourite food and tag along for the picnic. Where should all the ants be but in the picnic basket all along! This tale with similar refrains and the joke at the end will amuse.
*Macmillan* 🅷 5–7 years

### Arthur
*Amanda Graham, illustrated by Donna Gynell*
Poor Arthur is a rather ordinary dog in Mrs Humber's Pet Shop. All the other animals find homes but Arthur, even when he demonstrates he can act like a rabbit, snake or fish. One day a young girl asks for the extraordinary dog who performs tricks — it's Arthur!
*Era* 🅷 5–7 years ☆

### Brown Bear, Brown Bear, What Do You See?
*Bill Martin Jr, illustrated by Eric Carle*
A great rhyming, rhythmic text for the beginning reader, this story repeats the phrase, 'What do you see?' as each new animal appears in brightly coloured collage. The text then virtually reads without 'knowing' the words. There's the added anticipation of guessing what animal will appear next.
*Collins Lion* 🅿 3–6 years

### Clive Eats Alligators
*Alison Lester*
Seven highly individualistic children are illustrated, with a simple text, in daily activities. Six feature across a double-page spread, while the seventh on the following page offers a surprise. Clive is particularly fond of alligators and they feature in most scenes.
*Oxford University Press* 🅷 4–6 years ☆

### The Great Big Enormous Turnip
*Alexei Tolstoy, illustrated by Helen Oxenbury*
When an old man plants a little turnip and says, 'Grow sweet and strong', little does he realise how hard it will be to uproot. One after the other, he calls for the help of the old woman, granddaughter, dog, cat, mouse and at last they pull it up.
*Collins Lion* 🅿 4–6 years

### Hairy Maclary From Donaldson's Dairy
*Lynley Dodd*
An assorted collection of dogs out on the prowl meet up with 'Scarface Claw, the toughest Tom in town' who chases them home. As each animal joins the parade, a new rhyming couplet is added to the previous one making it great fun to read aloud. Tom's appearance is a terrific startler and will be looked forward to repeatedly.
*Puffin* 🅿 3–6 years

### Hattie And The Fox

*Mem Fox, illustrated by Patricia Mullins*

Lurking in the bushes is a fox and spying his presence is Hattie, the big black hen. As each part of the fox emerges, Hattie excitedly comments but the other farmyard animals are rather bored by it all until — pounce! The fox emerges. The repetition, drama and surprise make this perfect for the young. Tissue-paper illustrations are superb.
*Ashton Scholastic* **P** 2–5 years ☆

### The Napping House

*Audrey Wood, illustrated by Don Wood*

Here's a sleepy-time story with a difference. The entire family — mouse, cat, dog, child, granny — are napping peacefully until a pesky fly disturbs them. In an exciting series of events, text and illustrations reveal a huge mound of sleepers, a scene of silly and amusing humour.
*Dent* **H** 3–6 years

### What's The Time, Mr Wolf?

*Colin Hawkins*

From 7.00 am to 6.00 pm, the viewer participates in Mr Wolf's day, from brushing teeth to retiring to bed. Several of the double-page spreads feature pop-up illustrations, always those with a big surprise, such as Mr Wolf's large open mouth shouting he's ready for tea!
*Collins Lion* **P** 3–6 years

### My Cat Likes To Hide In Boxes

*Eve Sutton, illustrated by Lynley Dodd*

A variety of cats from different countries engage in amusing antics with one line repeated: 'But MY cat likes to hide in boxes'. Each new cat is introduced in a two-line rhyme which is then repeated in the following text. The predictable text and humorous illustrations are ideal for early and beginning readers.
*Puffin* **P** 2–5 years

### The Lighthouse Keeper's Lunch

*Ronda and David Armitage*

Each day, Mrs Grinling prepares a gourmet lunch for her husband, and sends it by a suspended wire from home to the lighthouse. Some enterprising seagulls enjoy these daily lunches until clever Mrs Grinling packs mustard sandwiches! Watercolour illustrations highlight this tale with balloon dialogue conversations between seagulls adding extra humour.
*Puffin* **P** 4–8 years

### Jump, Frog, Jump!

*Robert Kalan, illustrated by Byron Barton*

Frog's adventures in a pond are hazardous but in each case disaster is averted by the repeated simple action and refrain, 'Jump, frog, jump!' Frog escapes fish, snake, turtle, net and children all illustrated in a bold, simple and brightly coloured style.
*Scholastic* **P** 4–6 years

### Mr Gumpy's Outing

*John Burningham*

A classic, much-loved tale with elements of anticipation, repetition and humour. When Mr Gumpy takes his boat down the river, he agrees to take an assortment of animals with him, provided they behave. However havoc follows and all take a dunking, but swim ashore and arrive home in time for tea. Rich language and whimsical, humorous illustrations appeal.
*Puffin* **P** 3–6 years

### The Imaginary Menagerie

*Hazel Edwards*

No fears of the dark for this imaginative young lady who summons her nightly patrols of animals, birds and insects for protection! The antics of these mainly Australian creatures lighten the tale and the repeated refrain and rhythmic language make this a read-aloud specialty.
*Collins* **P** 5–7 years ☆

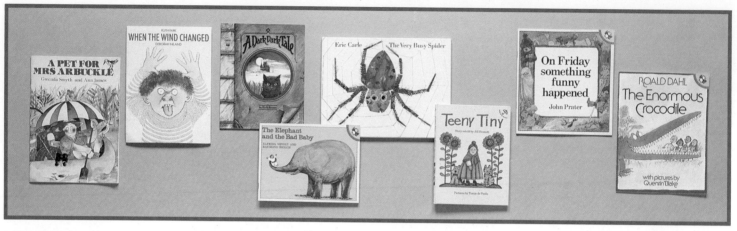

## A Dark Dark Tale
*Ruth Brown*
A spooky tale with its mood sustained by dark and eerie illustrations. A black cat progresses through dark, dark woods to a dark, dark house, door, hall, passage and room until a box appears. Suspense is beautifully built by the repetition of 'dark, dark . . .' and the accompanying strange illustrations. A surprise ending and release of tension!
*Scholastic* **P** 5–6 years

## The Elephant And The Bad Baby
*Elfrida Vipont, illustrated by Raymond Briggs*
One day an elephant and a bad baby go for a ride and together they take ice-creams, pies, biscuits, lollipops, apples and are subsequently chased by the vendors. But the bad baby never once says 'please' and gets his just desserts. This tale is much loved and each new reader invariably says, 'Again!'
*Puffin* **P** 2–5 years

## The Enormous Crocodile
*Roald Dahl, illustrated by Quentin Blake*
Dahl's quirky, black and dastardly humour. A crocodile makes secret plans and clever tricks in order to have delicious children for lunch. But each plan is foiled just in time so the crocodile deserves his fate.
*Puffin* **P** 6–9 years

## When The Wind Changed
*Ruth Park, illustrated by Deborah Niland*
There's an old saying that if you make faces and the wind changes, then you're stuck with that contortion! This disaster happens to young Josh but so frightening is his expression that he manages to frighten a bank robber and, with his father's help, becomes a hero. More horrific, grotesque faces you will not see.
*Collins* **P** 5–8 years ☆

## Teeny Tiny
*Retold by Jill Bennett, illustrated by Tomie de Paola*
A great ghost story for the youngest beginner reader. There was once a teeny tiny woman who lived in a teeny tiny house in a teeny tiny village — that sets the pattern for her trip to a graveyard where she picks up a bone intending to make a soup. That night a voice demands the bone back! The delight is twofold: the repetition in the text and the lurking ghosts.
*Oxford University Press* **P** 4–7 years

## The Very Busy Spider
*Eric Carle*
As a busy spider constructs her web, various animals invite her for adventures. The spider is much too busy to answer. Great book for participation: the web and spider are raised to the touch, the repetitive sentence structure and noisy animals all invite responses.
*Hamish Hamilton* **H** 2–5 years

## On Friday Something Funny Happened
*John Prater*
Two rabblerousing children spend each day of the week in misadventures. While the text is plain and simple, such as 'On Wednesday we did some painting', the wordless multiple frames reveal an absolute mess with paint on cats and teddies, walls and children! Children and adults alike will recognise familiar scenes.
*Puffin* **P** 6 + years

## A Pet For Mrs Arbuckle
*Gwenda Smyth, illustrated by Ann James*
Mrs Emmeline Arbuckle advertises for a pet and receives eleven applications from around the world. Accompanied by an adviser, the gingernut cat, Mrs Arbuckle interviews them all but finds each unsuitable. However, the gingernut agrees to be her pet.
*Ashton Scholastic* **P** 5–7 years ☆

# Beginning to read

These books are specifically designed to help children become fluent readers. They have simple words, clearly introduced so that their meaning is obvious; generous spacing between the lines; large print; wide margins and appealing illustrations which provide clues to what is happening in the text. These are books for children to read independently, but don't forget to continue reading books aloud which satisfy the demand for stories too difficult for children to read by themselves.

## Benny's Animals And How He Put Them In Order
*Millicent Selsam*
Benny enjoys putting every-thing in order and becomes absorbed in observing animals' characteristics. During the course of his study, he learns different ways to group animals through question-and-answer sessions with a professor at a museum. Sound dry? Not the way this tale is told and illustrated!
Also: *Terry And The Caterpillars; Egg To Chick; Greg's Microscope*
*Harper & Row* 🅷 5–8 years
(Library)

## The Case Of The Cat's Meow
*Crosby Bonsall*
Here's a story with spirit: a cat disappears and a clubhouse full of children set out to solve the mystery. There are a number of funny episodes before the problem eventually solves itself: the cat reappears with kittens!
Also: *The Day I Had To Play With My Baby Sister; And I Mean It Stanley; Who's Afraid Of The Dark?*
*World's Work* 🅷 6–8 years

## Little Chick's Breakfast
*Mary De Ball Kwitz*
Little Chick is eager for her favourite breakfast, but Broody Hen says they must wait for the sun to come up. One after the other, the farm animals get their breakfast and at last, Little Chick has hers, too! Nice sense of anticipation and a tale of impatience, a theme sure to be understood.
*World's Work* 🅷 5–8 years

## Amelia Bedelia Helps Out
*Peggy Parish*
Amelia Bedelia, a house and garden helper, has good intentions but misunderstands instructions. She weeds the garden by planting weeds, stakes the beans with juicy steak and makes tea cake with tea leaves! Word puns and silly misunderstandings have humorous appeal.
*Avon* 🅿
6–8 years

## Arthur's Honey Bear
*Lillian Hoban*
These sibling chimpanzees, Arthur and Violet, quickly become fast friends for the reader following their relationship and everyday adventures. Here Arthur decides to see his old Honey Bear.
Also: *Arthur's Prize Reader; Arthur's Penpal; Arthur's Christmas Cookies; Arthur's Funny Money*
*Harper & Row* 🅷 5–7 years

## Old Hat New Hat
*Stan and Jan Berenstain*
There's no difficulty in guessing the words in this funny story about selecting a hat. After help with a first reading, the rhyme and illustrations, which are clear clues to the text, should have beginners reading on their own.
*Collins* 🅿 4–6 years

## Commander Toad In Space
*Jane Yolen, illustrated by Bruce Degen*
A wonderfully silly take-off of *Star Wars* movies makes exciting science fiction for younger readers. Brave Commander Toad and his crew, Mr Hop, Lieutenant Lilly and Jack Skyjumper, fly their ship, *Star Warts,* into uncharted regions where they encounter Deep Wader. The usual galactic conflicts follow.
Also: *Commander Toad And The Planet Of The Grapes; Commander Toad And The Intergalactic Spy*
*Putnam* 🅿 5–7 years

## Spooky Riddles
*Marc Brown*
There are never enough riddles or spooky stories to satisfy children. 'What do bats need after a shower? Answer: a bat mat. How does a witch tell time? With a witchwatch.' Word plays abound and the comic illustrations add to the fun.
*Collins* 🅿 6–8 years

## Little Bear

*Else Holmelund Minarik,*
*illustrated by Maurice Sendak*
Here are four short stories
about Little Bear and his
mother. He is imaginative and
adventurous but never strays
far from home; she, under-
standingly, allows him
freedom and security. Among
his adventures are: dressing
for the snow, making birthday
soup, flying to the moon and
hearing about these past
events. Illustrations are very
expressive and appealing.
These long-time favourites
have simple but natural
language.
Also: *Father Bear Comes*
*Home*
*Puffin* P 6–8 years

## The Cat In The Hat

*Dr Seuss*
A winner with beginners —
the first of the Dr Seuss
beginner books. On a rainy
day, a mischievous cat pays
two children a visit and
creates havoc in the house
but miraculously cleans
up before mother arrives
home. Appeal is in the zany
antics, absurd drawings
and the repetitive, rhyming
text.
Also: *The Foot Book; Are You*
*My Mother; Go, Dog, Go; Ten*
*Apples Up On Top*
*Collins* P 4–6 years

## Oink And Pearl

*Kay Chorao*
In this story an affectionate
and secure family relationship
is portrayed. Oink is Pearl's
baby brother and they share
hurt feelings, physical bumps,
parties and visiting relatives.
These four short stories will be
within the young child's
understanding.
*Puffin* P 6–8 years

## Fox All Week

*Edward Marshall*
Fox and his friends Carmen,
the frog, and Dexter, the pig,
feature in these misadventures. Fox has a way of getting
into trouble but usually
winds up a winner. Included
here are stories of school,
girlfriends, cooking, visits
and reading, all with a
humorous twist. Each
page features coloured
zany illustrations matching
the text.
Also: *Fox And His Friends;*
*Fox In Love; Fox At School*
*Bodley Head* H 5–7 years
(Library)

## Grizzwold

*Syd Hoff*
Grizzwold is an old favourite,
a large friendly bear, left bereft
of his forest home when
loggers cut down the trees. He
tries to find a new home — a
zoo, a circus, and others — but
none satisfies until he finds a
safe forest reserve.
*Puffin* P 6–8 years

## Tales Of Oliver Pig

*Jean Van Leeuwen, illustrated*
*by Arnold Lobel*
The Benjamin Pig family is
warm and loving. Baby
Amanda and older brother
Oliver star in scenes from
daily life: making biscuits,
eating dinner, visiting
grandmother. Small line and
grey sketches add humour and
character.
Also: *More Tales Of Oliver*
*Pig; Amanda Pig And Her Big*
*Brother Oliver*
*Collins Lion* P 5–7 years

*There Is A Carrot In My Ear*

## Mouse Tales

*Arnold Lobel*
Papa Mouse tells seven
goodnight tales to his mice —
each tale is whimsical,
adventurous and humorous.
Text is repetitive without
being boring and stories are
simply written but not
bland. Illustrations, in small
coloured sketches, add
visual clues.
Also: *Mouse Soup*
*Puffin* P 6–8 years

## There Is A Carrot In My Ear And Other Noodle Tales
*Retold by Alvin Schwartz, illustrated by Karen Ann Weinhaus*
Noodle stories are about silly persons who do and say silly things. Here are six stories about a family of noodles. Simple sentences and a coloured illustration per page aid the beginner. These are tales from around the world.
*Scholastic* **P** 5–7 years

## Dinosaur Time
*Peggy Parish*
Dinosaurs are a top attraction for young children who are rarely daunted by the scientific names. This easy reader has short chapters on different dinosaurs. Illustrations add information on physical appearance, habitat and eating patterns. A brief introduction and ending suggest their living patterns and explain we know little about their extinction.
*World's Work* **P** 6–8 years

## It's Me, Hippo!
*Mike Thaler*
Hippo is endearing in these four short stories about finding a house, painting a picture, sharing the measles and having a birthday. The humour is light and the stories appealing with a number of jungle animals starring.
*World's Work* **H** 5–8 years

## Just Like That
*Mem Fox, illustrated by Kilmeny Niland*
Harriet Harris was horribly clumsy: knocking over juice, spilling jam, tearing overalls and much more. Her patient mother holds her temper by repeating a refrain, but the tension continues to build until she finally shouts! The appealing illustrations reveal all Harriet's difficulties and her mother's refrain is great for the beginning reader. There's a warm and comforting cuddle at the end.
*Hodder & Stoughton* **P** 5–8 years ☆

## Red Nose Readers
*Allan Ahlberg and Colin McNaughton*
This series for early readers has all the essential ingredients for appeal. There's humour of every type: absurdity, surprise, slapstick, verbal and visual humour, and several stories built on familiar nursery rhymes and stories. Illustrations feature monsters galore and action aplenty.
*Walker* **H** 4–6 years

## The Tale Of Thomas Mead
*Pat Hutchins*
Thomas Mead, who can't read, finds himself in great trouble when he goes into ladies' restrooms, pushes the wrong buttons, and walks on the wrong traffic signal which lands him in gaol. There he finally learns to read! A rhyming test, additional dialogue, and illustrations of catastrophes all add up to a humorous tale with a message.
*Pan* **P** 5–8 years

## The Story Of Bentley Beaver
*Marjorie Weinman Sharmat*
For children who are mystified by succeeding generations, this tale of Bentley Beaver growing up, getting married, having children and grandchildren and growing old, is a gem. There's much family tradition here: sayings, songs and many interests carried through the generations.
*World's Work* **H** 5–8 years

## Frog And Toad Are Friends
*Arnold Lobel*
Two best friends, Frog and Toad, share the beginning of spring, stories, lost belongings and a swim together. All ages will recognise the emotions here in these four short stories about friendship and sharing. The whimsical, softly coloured illustrations are perfect.
Also: *Frog And Toad All Year*
*Puffin* **P** 6–8 years

# Developing readers

There is a point in time when the child who can read independently feels ready for more than a picture book but a novel looks too daunting. These books form a bridge to more advanced reading. Often they are liberally illustrated (resting points after lots of print), divided into short, manageable chapters and are not too long. Above all, these books have high appeal with humour a frequent ingredient to lighten the process of reading and to ensure that reading remains an enjoyable experience.

### Annie And The Old One
*Miska Miles, illustrated by Peter Parnall*
Annie struggles against her grandmother's assertion that her time to die will coincide with the completion of a new rug being woven on her mother's loom. Surreptitiously Annie unravels the weaving nightly, but her grandmother helps her understand and accept the natural cycle of life and death. The traditions of the Navaho Indians are beautifully revealed in this gentle story and expressive illustrations.
*Little, Brown* **P** 7–10 years

### The Battle Of Bubble And Squeak
*Philippa Pearce, illustrated by Alan Baker*
No animal lover should miss this suspenseful tale of children battling against their mother who rejects their two pet gerbils. When Ginger the cat injures poor Bubble, a dose of antibiotics three times a day is the only cure and mother comes around, proving most dexterous at administering the vital medicine. All ends satisfyingly with the thought of baby gerbils on the horizon.
*Puffin* **P** 9–12 years

### Nate The Great
*Marjorie Weinman Sharmat, illustrated by Marc Simont*
Boy detective, Nate the Great, dresses in Sherlock Holmes attire, and sets out to recover a mystery painting. Deadpan humour and exciting exploits keep readers clamouring for more of these lightweight, easy-to-read mysteries.
*World's Work* **H** 8–10 years

### The Red Balloon
*Albert Lamorisse*
A lonely French boy, Pascal, befriends a red balloon which follows him everywhere. When some rough boys try to steal this magical balloon, tragedy strikes and the balloon bursts. Amazingly, the sky fills with balloons and together they take Pascal on a trip around the world. A classic, highly appealing story.
*Doubleday* **P** 5–9 years

### Betsy-Tacy
*Maud Hart Lovelace, illustrated by Lois Lenski*
Betsy and Tacy are five-year-old inseparable friends. While set in a small Minnesota town in the early 1900s, their everyday lives — a new baby, losing a baby-sitter and so on — are recognisable and enjoyed today. A warm friendship pervades this and the sequels in which the girls mature.
*Harper & Row* **P** 7–9 years

### Through Grandpa's Eyes
*Patricia MacLachlan, illustrated by Deborah Ray*
John learns to experience life as his blind grandfather does: smelling breakfast and flowers, hearing birds fly, and feeling faces with fingers. A gentle, understanding text and soft pastel watercolours blend perfectly to give an insight into a blind person's experience of life.
*Harper & Row* **P** 7–9 years

### Daggie Dogfoot
*Dick King-Smith, illustrated by Mary Rayner*
Daggie Dogfoot, born on an English pig farm, earns his nickname because his front trotters resemble paws. After misinterpreting an overheard comment that pigs might fly, Daggie sets out to do just that. Witty writing, comical scenes and excellent characterisation win this author readers.
*Puffin* **P** 9–11 years

### The Whipping Boy
*Sid Fleischman, illustrated by Peter Sis*
A popular teller of humorous tall tales offers a zany plot with surprises galore. Prince Brat runs away taking his whipping boy who must endure all the punishments earned by the mischievous prince. Adventures on the road along with a host of colourful characters make this an enjoyable, easy-to-read short novel.
*Greenwillow* **H** 9–11 years

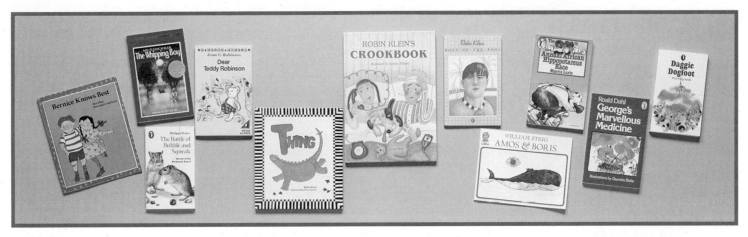

## Robin Klein's Crookbook
*Robin Klein, illustrated by Kristen Hilliard*
A how-to-do-it book with suggestions for being thoroughly obnoxious and troublesome at home, school and hospital. The humour, brevity and amusing illustrations will attract the poor, as well as the good, reader.
*Methuen* 🅗 8–12 years ☆

## Thing
*Robin Klein, illustrated by Alison Lester*
Because Emily Forbes lives in a flat she is not allowed a pet, so a seemingly harmless rock appears a suitable substitute until it hatches into a baby stegosaurus! How Emily camouflages her pet and how 'Thing' becomes a hero makes a very amusing and appealing tale.
Sequel: *Thingnapped!*
*Oxford University Press* 🅟
7–9 years ☆

## The Twenty-Seventh Annual African Hippopotamus Race
*Morris Lurie, illustrated by Elizabeth Honey*
Edward, our hero, is eight years old and in training for an annual swimming event. All aspects of Edward's training are hilariously sketched and the reader cheers for this two-and-a-half-tonne athlete. It appears poor sportsmanship will win over honest Edward but in a rip-roaring conclusion, the good wins out. A favourite.
*Puffin* 🅟 7–9 years ☆

## Bernice Knows Best
*Max Dann, illustrated by Ann James*
Everyone avoids Hugh for catastrophes dog his path. That is until he meets Bernice who sees his bungling as a challenge to cure. Playful, humorous illustrations on every page are perfect for this tale.
*Oxford University Press* 🅟
7–9 years ☆

## Boss Of The Pool
*Robin Klein*
Shelley's mother works as an occupational therapy aide at a hostel for the disabled, but her daughter objects to being near those different from herself. When she finds the hostel's swimming pool, Shelley comes inside and discovers Ben, who is petrified of water. She sees his fear as a challenge to overcome and in dispelling Ben's phobia she develops an understanding of the disabled in a natural, satisfying way.
*Omnibus* 🅗 8–10 years ☆

## George's Marvellous Medicine
*Roald Dahl, illustrated by Quentin Blake*
George's grandmother is irritable and bossy and one day, particularly so. George concocts a special medicine bound to either cure her or explode her away!
But the magic brings unexpected results.
*Puffin* 🅟 8–10 years

## Amos And Boris
*William Steig*
A moving story of friendship. Amos builds a boat and goes to sea where Boris, a whale, rescues him from a major catastrophe. Years later, Boris is beached by an horrific storm and it is Amos's turn to save his friend's life. The language and vocabulary are rich and suited to an able reader.
*Collins Lion* 🅟 7–9 years
(Library)

## Dear Teddy Robinson
*Joan G Robinson*
Teddy-bear lovers will enjoy these eight tales of Teddy Robinson. Though Teddy never actively participates in adventures, he is thoroughly involved in household affairs, such as watching the toast and keeping the house. Easy-to-read text with amusing small poems are all made more appealing by the line illustrations of Teddy and his owner Deborah.
*Puffin* 🅟 7–9 years

### The Vanishment Of Thomas Tull

*Janet and Allan Ahlberg*
Thomas Tull has great problems, he shrinks then grows to giant proportions. All the contraptions and concoctions used to cure his problem are amply described and illustrated in minute detail. Throughout there are drawings of predicaments and unusual characters and the text features posters, notes and framed comic adventures. A read-aloud delight for its rich language. Developing readers will enjoy the humour and illustrations which help in story development.
*Puffin* P 7–9 years

### Sarah, Plain And Tall

*Patricia MacLachlan*
Sarah, plain and tall, answers an advertisement in the newspaper for a wife and mother. When she arrives for a visit, young Caleb and Anna quickly grow to love her strong, warm personality. Even Papa sings as he once used to do. But one day Sarah takes the wagon into town and all fear she will leave for her home — Maine and the sea. She returns and confesses that though she will always miss her home, she would miss her family more. A mood of warmth and security surrounds this affectionate family story. With easy-to-read language rich in visual imagery, this short novel is a joy to read.
*Julia MacRae* P 8–10 years

### McBroom And The Great Race

*Sid Fleischman, illustrated by Quentin Blake*
Josh McBroom lives on a 'spanglorious' farm where tall tales are everyday events. In this story, a giant rooster and a jackalope (cross between a jack rabbit and an antelope) race. The stakes are high: McBroom may lose his farm to the sly Heck Jones. But clever thinking and a number of improbable events ensure the better man wins. Line illustrations perfectly suit this rollicking tale.
Also: *Here Comes McBroom's Ghost; McBroom's Zoo; McBroom Tells The Truth Chatto and Windus* H
7–10 years (Library)

### Jacob Two-Two Meets The Hooded Fang

*Mordecai Richler, illustrated by Fritz Wegner*
Jacob, aged six, has two elder brothers and two elder sisters and suffers from extreme shyness and an inferiority complex. His practice of repeating everything twice to make himself heard lands him in big trouble when he is incarcerated in Children's Prison. There he discovers some two hundred other children and the frightening Hooded Fang who turns out to be devoted to children. An amusing tall tale about being small in a big world.
Also: *Jacob Two-Two And The Dinosaur*
*Puffin* P 7–11 years

### Penny Pollard's Diary

*Robin Klein, illustrated by Ann James*
Penny Pollard is a crusty, independent girl whose humorous exploits appeal to boys and girls alike. In her diary, she records in natural language her hatred of Annette Smurton and all elderly people. Her attitudes change though in a natural, satisfying way. Most appealing is the innovative format which includes snapshots, scribbles and simple drawings much as a 'real' Penny Pollard might create.
Also: *Penny Pollard's Letters; Penny Pollard In Print; Penny Pollard's Passport*
*Oxford University Press* P
8–12 years ☆

### Clever Polly And The Stupid Wolf

*Catherine Storr, illustrated by Marjorie-Ann Watts*
The wolf, intent on eating Clever Polly, is constantly foiled by his own lack of brains and Polly's resourceful nature. Many of these tales draw on familiar nursery rhymes and stories and children's games, and these parallels add appeal for the reader who can predict the likely catastrophe to come. The humorous jokes played on the wolf are cleverly constructed and the writing style is comfortable for developing readers.
*Puffin* P 8–10 years

### The Fiend Next Door

*Sheila Lavelle, illustrated by Linda Burch*
Charlie (Charlotte) Ellis lives next door to Angela Mitchell and they are usually best friends in spite of the fact that Angela's mischievous pranks invariably land Charlie in trouble. Kidnapping babies, locking teachers in sheds and making foxes into pets are just some of these episodic scrapes. These are tales of everyday life — home, school and friends — and have great appeal in an easy-to-read style.
Also: *My Best Fiend; Trouble With The Fiend*
*Collins Lion* P 9–11 years

### Ramona The Pest

*Beverly Cleary, illustrated by Louis Darling*
No child should miss Ramona Quimby who begins her school days as a kindergarten dropout then goes on to achieve much at home, school and community. Her insatiable curiosity, determination and assertive personality get her into many humorous scrapes. Over the years in this series, Ramona tackles friends, parents and teachers with her usual overzealous, bubbly enthusiasm. A well-loved series.
Also: *Ramona The Brave; Ramona Quimby, Age 8; Ramona And Her Father; Ramona And Her Mother; Ramona Forever*
*Puffin* P 7–9 years

### Fantastic Mr Fox
*Roald Dahl, illustrated by Jill Bennett*
Mr and Mrs Fox and their four youngsters live in a hole on the hill and acquire their food from three very mean farmers. Fed up with their food being stolen, the farmers wait outside the fox's hole determined to end his pilfering forever. Excellent illustrations, short chapters, an easy-to-read text and an exciting plot make this an ideal book for developing readers.
*Puffin* **P** 7–9 years

### One Night At Lottie's House
*Max Dann, illustrated by David Pearson*
Arthur always packs his ghost-fighting kit when spending a night away from home. Lottie's house is the spookiest by far and Arthur concocts a magical potion to ward off demons.
*Oxford University Press* **H**
7–9 years ☆

### Flat Stanley
*Jeff Brown, illustrated by Tomi Ungerer*
Imagine being as thin as a centimetre! Such is Flat Stanley's permanent condition after being squashed by a falling bulletin board. It's rather handy when Stanley can be rolled up and easily carried. Stanley's appearance is particularly useful in capturing art thieves. A long-time favourite, *Flat Stanley* is comically illustrated.
*Magnet* **P** 5–8 years

### Pigs Might Fly
*Emily Rodda, illustrated by Noela Young*
Rachel finds her boring existence completely overthrown when she is magically transported to a land of flying pigs and 'grunter' storms where unlikely behaviour is the norm. The sparkling prose and inventive plot is enhanced by line illustrations.
*Puffin* **P** 9–11 years ☆

### Jumanji
*Chris Van Allsburg*
This haunting fantasy lingers in the imagination. Two children find a board game, designed for the 'bored and restless'. The instructions rule that it must be played until one player reaches Jumanji, the garden city. With each throw of the dice, a bizarre event occurs. Realistic black-and-white illustrations draw the reader into the story. A surprise ending leaves the reader stunned.
*Houghton Mifflin* **H**
6–10 years

### All About Anna And Harriet And Christopher And Me
*Elizabeth Hathorn, illustrated by Stephen Axelsen*
Anna consistently turns daily life into one humorous catastrophe after another. This easy-to-read novel will appeal to children who enjoy the funny side of daily life.
*Methuen* **P** 9–11 years ☆

### Looking Out For Sampson
*Elizabeth Hathorn, illustrated by Ann James*
Looking after a younger brother can sometimes be a burden. When Bronwyn loses her younger brother at the beach she realises just how much she loves him. Feelings of jealousy, frustration, self-doubt and warming love are all sensitively treated.
*Oxford University Press* **H**
7–9 years ☆

### The Magic Finger
*Roald Dahl, illustrated by Pat Marriott*
Imagine a magical finger that transforms things at the whim of a young girl! Angered by the Gregg family's thoughtless hunting for pleasure, the young girl changes the Greggs' arms to wings and the ducks' wings to hands. When the ducks bring out guns to shoot the Greggs, the humans see the error of their ways.
*Puffin* **P** 7–9 years

# Poetry

Nursery rhymes provided your baby's first introduction to poetry. Even at a very young age, children respond to the rhythm and rhyme in poetry. Try a poem presented in picture-book form or dip into some of the wonderful poetry collections on such favourite subjects as dinosaurs or bushrangers. Sample the range of poetry from the breathtaking haiku and the visually appealing concrete poem to the rollicking ballad and ridiculously funny limerick. Be sure to select those that appeal to you because poetry works its best magic when read aloud with feeling!

## Talking To The Sun
*Compiled by Kenneth Koch and Kate Farrell, illustrated by Metropolitan Museum of Art (New York)*
This innovative anthology combines artwork from the New York Metropolitan Museum of Art with wide-ranging poems. African chants, European lullabies, American Indian verse and others feature in ten thematic sections. The dates of both poetry and art are included and offer some unusual combinations.
*Viking Kestrel* 🄷 9 + years

## Days Are Where We Live And Other Poems
*Compiled by Jill Bennett, illustrated by Maureen Roffey*
These twenty-four brief, whimsical poems are ideal to follow nursery rhymes. Everyday subjects such as baths, washing hair, new clothes and bedtime are all treated in clear, rhythmic language by contemporary poets Jack Prelutsky, Michael Rosen, John Ciardi, Aileen Fisher and others. Illustrations match perfectly.
Also: *Roger Was A Razor Fish*
*Bodley Head* 🄷 5–7 years (Library)

## Here A Little Child I Stand
*Cynthia Mitchell, illustrated by Satomi Ichikawa*
Simple, religious poems from various cultures with watercolour illustrations which capture the diverse settings and show the universal aspects of worship.
*Heinemann* 🄷 5–8 years

## Dreadful David
*Sally Odgers, illustrated by Craig Smith*
Every naughty child will identify with David's doings. On a visit to Gran's, he is an absolute horror, and Gran puts him to bed after terrible misdeeds. But note the gentle kiss when David is tucked in bed at last. The poetry is rhythmic and has a good pace for the various adventures. Excellent read aloud and the full-page illustrations reveal David's horrible misbehaviour.
*Omnibus* 🄿 4–7 years ☆

## All Small
*David McCord, illustrated by Madelaine Gill Linden*
A popular children's poet's work from several earlier books are collected here. The emphasis is on short poems with a child's perception. Delicate watercolours suit these poems.
*Little, Brown* 🄿 4–8 years (Library)

## When Did You Last Wash Your Feet?
*Michael Rosen, illustrated by Tony Pinchuck*
Subversive, outrageous, provocative — these poems are presented in a pop-art magazine style which will appeal to the less-than-avid reader or lukewarm fan of poetry. 'Spots', parents, ecology and politics: no subject is too sacred for the witty Rosen.
*Collins Lion* 🄿 9–15 years

## Peacock Pie
*Walter de la Mare, illustrated by Barbara Cooney*
An English poet of renown, Walter de la Mare's work should be a part of every child's experience. This collection is considered his best and is illustrated with pencil drawings which suit the mood.
*Faber & Faber* 🄿 8–10 years

## I Rhyme My Time: A Selection Of Poems For Young People
*David Martin, illustrated by Robert Ingpen*
Thought-provoking, amusing and lighthearted — there is poetry here to suit all moods. The philosophical and practical exist side by side: poems on peace, death, and eternity adjacent to those on policewomen, detectives and children. Evocative and realistic illustrations.
*Jacaranda* 🄷 10–15 years (Library) ☆

## Each Peach Pear Plum
*Janet and Allan Ahlberg*
A host of familiar characters from traditional tales are partially hidden, encouraging a game of 'I spy'. The story is more fun if the viewer knows the hidden characters but still the rhymed couplets give sufficient hints. Each couplet reveals the character from the previous page and the illustration opposite gives the next object to find. Many humorous details in the illustrations. The rhyme is part of schoolchildren's lore.
*Collins Lion* **P** 3–6 years

## A Paddock Of Poems
*Max Fatchen*
A popular Australian poet produces his third collection for children which is just as appealing as the others. Riddles, jokes, limericks, jingles and a range of poetic forms are all delivered in light-hearted style.
*Puffin* **P** 8–12 years ☆

## A Child's Garden Of Verses
*Robert Louis Stevenson, illustrated by Michael Foreman*
Stevenson's verse, first published in 1885, still holds charm for contemporary children especially with illustrations which capture both historical and contemporary times. Many of the verses will be familiar to adults and evoke fond memories to share.
*Gollancz* **H** 7–12 years

## All Asleep
*Charlotte Pomerantz, illustrated by Nancy Tafuri*
This collection of fifteen lullaby poems is perfect for sleepless children. The subjects of the poems are appealing, too: bees, dogs, sheep, children and so on. Nancy Tafuri specialises in books for the very young and her illustrations are simple, uncluttered and warm.
*Julia MacRae* **H** 3–6 years

## For Me, Me, Me: Poems For The Very Young
*Dorothy Butler (ed)*
A perfect collection for graduates of nursery rhymes. Each poem is brief and brisk, and many feature repetition and clear rhythm. Familiar poets included are:
R L Stevenson, James Reeves, Odgen Nash, Aileen Fisher plus many anonymous well-known rhymes. Small pencil illustrations are nice accompaniments. An index of authors, titles and first lines is included.
*Hodder & Stoughton* **H**
4–8 years

## In The Garden Of Bad Things
*Doug MacLeod, illustrated by Peter Thomson*
Twenty humorous poems have subjects of instant appeal: vampires, snakes, sharks, piranhas and dinosaurs. Soft pastel and line illustrations are a perfect match.
*Puffin* **P** 7 + years ☆

## Far Out, Brussel Sprout!
*Compiled by June Factor, illustrated by Peter Viska*
These are playground chants and games, skipping rhymes and poetry 'owned', devised and revised by children themselves. Often racy and just that little bit naughty, these poems never fail to please. Illustrated with humorous line drawings.
Also: *All Right, Vegemite Oxford University Press* **P**
7–12 years ☆

## The Night Before Christmas
*Clement C Moore, illustrated by James Marshall*
There are many illustrated versions of this world-famous poem originally published in 1822. This delightful edition shows a house full of animals and children all snugly settled down for the night. The bright, colourful illustrations are full of amusing details for children to enjoy.
*Scholastic* **P** 6–9 years

## Songs For My Dog And Other People

*Max Fatchen, illustrated by Michael Atchison*
Light and amusing poetry which appeals to all ages — for here is human nature. One amusing section is 'Nutty nursery rhymes', where you'll meet Miss Muffett who repels the spider with her pressurised spray. Michael Atchison, former Punch cartoonist, adds to the hilarity with zany illustrations.
*Kestrel* 🅷 9–11 years (Library) ☆

## Noah's Ark

*Translated by Peter Spier*
Spier uses a sixteenth century Dutch poem of this familiar biblical story as a base for watercolour illustrations appearing in sixty-three wordless frames crammed with details. Each illustration tells its own story of the difficulties of this voyage and the joyful relief when life begins again on land.
*Doubleday* 🅿 6–9 years

## You Can't Catch Me!

*Michael Rosen, illustrated by Quentin Blake*
Family life, food, and imaginative adventures abound. Throughout are zany, whimsical coloured illustrations, often several to a page. The book has been imaginatively and appealingly designed. Twenty-two poems feature, including both older and newer poets.
*Andre Deutsch* 🅷 7–9 years

## Hiawatha

*Henry Wadsworth Longfellow, illustrated by Susan Jeffers*
This epic poem was first published in 1855 and weaves together myths, legends and first-hand accounts of Hiawatha, an American Indian chief of the Onondaga tribe, who was known for his role in forming the Iroquois nation. Only those verses which deal with Hiawatha's childhood are illustrated. The lyrical verses are serious in tone but reveal a young child's delight and love of nature and animals. Delicately coloured, superb illustrations in a large format book are authentic, cultural portraits.
*Hamish Hamilton* 🅷 8–10 years (Library)

## I'll Tell You A Tale: A Collection Of Poems And Ballads

*Author and compiler Ian Serraillier*
An excellent collection of memorable English and Scottish traditional ballads and songs plus a number of poems, riddles and spells by Serraillier himself — a master of prose and verse. Subjects such as jealousy, death, love, betrayal, battles and murders are treated with sophistication. Illustrations include both black-and-white photographs and mysterious, evocative drawings by four different, well-chosen artists.
*Puffin* 🅿 10–15 years (Library)

## Poems For Over 10-Year-Olds

*Compiled by Kit Wright, illustrated by Michael Foreman*
Wright, a poet himself, offers a collection of well-known English and American poets, both older and contemporary. Story poems, such as 'The Highwayman' and 'The Shooting of Dan McGrew', are included along with cautionary tales, riddles, puns and a liberal sprinkling of eerie poems.
*Puffin* 🅿 10–15 years

## When We Were Very Young

*A A Milne, illustrated by E H Shepard*
No child should miss these whimsical and wonderfully rhythmic poems. So familiar are many of them that they form a common cultural heritage, complemented by the equally much-loved illustrations. Several of these poems have been reissued as separate picture books.
*Methuen* 🅿 7–10 years ☆

## I Like This Poem

*Kaye Webb (ed)*
An unusual collection compiled from one thousand children's recommendations solicited as a competition in England's Puffin Club. The collection is divided into age categories and each poem includes the child's recommendation. Choices are generally well-established poets of high standing.
*Puffin* 🅿 5–15 years

## Mister Magnolia

*Quentin Blake*
Here is zany nonsense in both text and inimitable Quentin Blake whimsical illustrations. Though Mr Magnolia may only have one boot, a key phrase repeated throughout, an array of rhyming events adds to the fun. The enormous variety of words rhyming with 'boot' will amaze and delight. Children will enjoy the repetition, participation, rhythm and rhyme.
*Collins* 🅿 5–7 years

## Sir Cedric

*Roy Gerrard*
Sir Cedric the knight is modest and polite and only fights in dire circumstances, such as defeating the bully Black Ned and rescuing a chubby but lovable princess. This amusing tale is told in rollicking verse with a dash of satire. Illustrations show a rather dumpy, balding Sir Cedric amidst ornately designed pages which invite close scrutiny.
*Gollancz* 🅷 6–9 years

## The New Kid On The Block

*Jack Prelutsky, illustrated by James Stevenson*
Prelutsky is one of America's most popular contemporary children's poets. This collection of one hundred witty and humorous poems is imaginatively and suitably extended by James Stevenson's equally quirky illustrations. Title and first line indexes.
*Greenwillow* 🅷 9–11 years

## The Oath Of Bad Brown Bill

*Stephen Axelsen*
No one was safe from the
marauding bushranger Bad
Brown Bill until he met his
match — monster ghosts! The
poetic language is suitably foul
and loathsome in tone just as
the illustrations are dark and
wonderfully ghoulish.
Reading this poem aloud
brings out its strong visual
images and rollicking rhythm.
*Puffin* **P** 7–9 years ☆

## Oxford Book Of Poetry For Children

*Compiled by Edward Blishen,
illustrated by
Brian Wildsmith*
This large anthology offers an
excellent introduction to the
best of English poets.
A wide range of subjects
and poetic forms are included,
all handsomely illustrated in
brilliant colours. Author and
first line indexes are included.
*Oxford University Press* **P**
9–12 years

## Quick, Let's Get Out Of Here

*Michael Rosen, illustrated by
Quentin Blake*
The combined wit of Rosen
and Blake make this an
uproarious collection, enticing
even those uninterested in
poetry. Long story poems, short
cryptic poems and poems of
everyday life all feature.
*Puffin* **P** 9–11 years

## Rattling In The Wind: Australian Poetry For Children

*Compiled by Jill Heylen and
Celia Jellett, illustrated by
Maire Smith*
Over ninety poems by both
established and emerging
Australian poets are included
in this handsome anthology
illustrated in a striking,
photographic style. Themes
cover the child's personal
world, the wider environment
and world concerns. Notable
inclusions are Aboriginal and
children's poetry.
*Omnibus* **H** 9–12 years ☆

## Sing A Song Of Popcorn

*Beatrice Schenk de Regniers,
and other selectors*
Nine highly acclaimed
illustrators contribute to this
collection of nine thematic
areas of poetry including
weather, rhymes, feelings,
animals, people, nonsense,
spooky things and stories. The
poets represent the past and
present. The poems have
proven their appeal. Now
coupled with illustrators of
the calibre of Leo and Diane
Dillon, Arnold Lobel, and
Maurice Sendak, amongst
others, each receives a new life.
*Scholastic* **P** 8 + years

## Tiny Tim: Verses For Children

*Compiled by Jill Bennett,
illustrated by Helen Oxenbury*
Twenty short poems by well-
known poets are included for
the young. Some are excellent
for finger puppets, others for
choral reading and chanting.
Illustrations are appealing.
*Collins Lion* **P** 3–6 years

## The Walker Book Of Read-Aloud Rhymes For The Very Young

*Jack Prelutsky (ed), illustrated
by Marc Brown*
A poet himself, Prelutsky
selects over two hundred
verses from one hundred
poets for this exceptional
collection. A variety of
lengths, rhythms and rhyming
schemes are included, and
each is a read-aloud delight.
Themes familiar to childhood
abound, all enhanced
by exuberant and humorous
artwork on well-designed pages.
*Walker* **H** 3–8 years

## Tyrannosaurus Was A Beast

*Jack Prelutsky, illustrated by
Arnold Lobel*
Fourteen dinosaur
personalities are captured in
brief often witty verse. Not
only will children take the
subject to heart but enjoy the
poetry and learn some natural
history in this collection.
*Walker* **H** 7–10 years

### Mulga Bill's Bicycle

*A B Paterson, illustrated by Deborah and Kilmeny Niland*
Few illustrators could capture this rollicking humorous tale so effectively. Mulga Bill gives away his horse for a bicycle, but a sound dousing in the creek convinces him to ride his horse again.
*Collins* 🅿 8–12 years ☆

### If I Were In Charge Of The World And Other Worries

*Judith Viorst*
The author has a way of pinpointing children's concerns in a humorous way and always prods us to laugh at ourselves. These forty-one poems cover such areas as wishes and worries, facts of life and 'wicked thoughts' and are unfailingly bright and optimistic. Contrasting illustrations add another feature.
*Ashton Scholastic* 🅿
7–10 years

### Sister Madge's Book Of Nuns

*Doug MacLeod, illustrated by Craig Smith*
This collection of riotously funny poems leads the reader to believe they are written by Sister Madge from the Convent of Our Lady of Immense Proportions. But whoever met nuns riding motorbikes down supermarket aisles? This scene and many others are captured by an artist who matches the poet for sheer zany humour.
*Omnibus* 🅷 9 + years ☆

### Someone Is Flying Balloons

*Compiled by Jill Heylen and Celia Jellett, illustrated by Kerry Argent*
An all-Australian collection featuring poems of the child's imagination and the wider world, with the emphasis on joy, humour and self-awareness. Beautifully detailed, realistic illustrations throughout.
*Omnibus* 🅷 9–12 years ☆

### Sir Francis Drake: His Daring Deeds

*Roy Gerrard*
Rhymed couplets humorously trace Drake's encounters with the Spanish, battles with violent storms and his eventual knighthood. The intricately detailed and authentic settings and costumes are an added bonus to this tongue-in-cheek historical adventure.
*Gollancz* 🅷 7–10 years

### When A Goose Meets A Moose

*Compiled by Clare Scott-Mitchell, illustrated by Louise Hogan*
A selection of over one hundred short poems by mainly British and American poets aimed at children from toddler through primary age. Illustrations throughout make this an attractive collection. Author and first line indexes. Also: *Apples From Hurricane Street*
*Hamlyn* 🅷 6–10 years

### The Walker Book Of Poetry For Children

*Jack Prelutsky (ed), illustrated by Arnold Lobel*
An excellent bumper collection of 572 poems for primary school children. Prelutsky is a respected children's poet himself and this selection represents poems he has found appealing on school visits. Fourteen sections include many topics of interest to children such as nonsense, food, dogs and cats, bears and bats. Arnold Lobel's whimsical illustrations suit this light and humorous collection. Title, author, subject and first line indexes.
*Walker* 🅷 5–10 years

*If I Were In Charge Of The World*

# Anthologies

These collections provide a tempting variety of literature for all ages. Sample nursery stories from those specially selected and presented for children under five. Older readers can try stories by different authors, parts of longer works or different types of literature such as verse, short stories, plays or songs. Anthologies make convenient reading, too, for those who simply want a short and enjoyable reading experience.

## Guardian Angels: Fifteen New Stories By Winners Of The Guardian Children's Fiction Award

*Stephanie Nettel (ed), illustrated by Mike Daley*
Often a collection of short stories has only some very good tales, the difference here is that each story is by a fine storyteller who offers a distinctive style and a fascinating tale. Authors such as K M Peyton, Leon Garfield and Peter Dickinson appear and so the range of stories is also wide — historical fiction, supernatural, science fiction and animal stories are examples. The collection makes great read-aloud sessions and is also useful to discover new authors.
*Viking* ⊞ 10–12 years

## Gold And Silver, Silver And Gold: Tales Of Hidden Treasure

*Alvin Schwartz, illustrated by David Christiana*
The author specialises in folklore and here has an irresistible collection. Legends, tall tales and true stories all concern treasure. Not only do these tales cover the backyard variety of treasure but offer clues to treasures that are yet to be found. The black-and-white illustrations create just the right atmosphere.
*Farrar, Straus & Giroux* ⊞ 9–12 years

## The Nursery Story Book

*Kay Chorao*
This collection of thirteen stories includes well-known ones such as 'The Three Bears' and two long story rhymes. Language and plots are simple and design and illustrations are superb, altogether creating a cosy, warm mood.
*Collins* ⊞ 4–7 years

## Juba This And Juba That

*Virginia A Tashjian*
A much-flavoured collection of rhymes, stories, songs, chants and jokes all designed for children to join in. Appropriate to a wide age range including some for babies then up to mid-primary years. Generally for parents to use with children.
Also: *With A Deep Sea Smile*
*Longman Young* ⊞ 7–10 years (Library)

## Taking The Chook And Other Traumas Of Growing Up

*Jean Holkner*
Growing up Jewish during the Depression in Carlton, Victoria, is revealed in these fourteen short stories. The sharp and humorous observations of life will appeal to many ages. The writing style is lively, simple and filled with plenty of dialogue, thus making these stories easy to read and enjoy.
*Puffin* ⊞ 10 + years ☆

## Eric Carle's Treasury Of Classic Stories For Children

*Eric Carle*
Twenty-two stories by Aesop and Hans Christian Andersen, plus collected tales from the brothers Grimm, are included in this sumptuously illustrated anthology. Each tale is retold in appealing read-aloud prose and illustrated in colour by this master of the collage artistic technique.
*Orchard* ⊞ 5–9 years

## The Fairy Tale Treasury

*Selected by Virginia Haviland, illustrated by Raymond Briggs*
Thirty-two favourite stories are included such as 'Jack and the Beanstalk', 'The Ugly Duckling' and 'Cinderella'. Jamaican, African, Danish, English, German, Spanish and Russian tales feature. Illustrations decorate the margins and feature as full pages.
*Hamish Hamilton* ⊞ 3–7 years

## Tomie de Paola's Favourite Nursery Tales

*Illustrated by Tomie de Paola*
A large, lavishly illustrated anthology of many old favourites and some new tales. The brothers Grimm, Aesop, and poets such as R L Stevenson, William Longfellow and Edmund Lear are all included. The illustrations of these thirty tales and poems are superb.
*Methuen* ⊞ 6–10 years (Library)

### The Helen Oxenbury Nursery Story Book
*Helen Oxenbury*
Here are ten of the most familiar and appropriate tales for the youngest, including 'The Three Billy Goats Gruff', 'The Little Red Hen', and 'Goldilocks'. Coloured illustrations and simple language in large type make it a pleasure to read. 'The Three Little Pigs' is a shortened version and in 'Little Red Riding Hood', girl and grandma pop out of the wolf, none the worse for their adventure.
*Heinemann*  3–7 years

### Ratbags And Rascals
*Robin Klein, illustrated by Alison Lester*
Seventeen stories feature a range of offbeat characters in zany situations: a kidnapping with the victim in charge, pirates and robots. Small line drawings appear throughout these humorous tales.
*Dent* 8–11 years ☆

### The Illustrated Treasury Of Australian Stories And Verse For Children
*Compiled by Barbara Ker Wilson*
An excellent collection of Australian verse and excerpts from novels which span the years from 1854 to 1984. Included are brief biographies of authors and numerous illustrations to convey this art form's historical development.
*Nelson* 9 + years ☆

### Unreal! Eight Surprising Stories
*Paul Jennings*
Irresistible, belly-laughing humour in these eight tales. Ghostly bones that seek reunion; magical lipsticks that win kisses; smart aleck ice-cream that makes eaters dumb — these and more appear. Simple language, clever plots and zany characters have great appeal.
*Puffin* 10 + years ☆

### A Teddy Bear's Picnic
*Illustrated by Terry Denton*
These stories will have great appeal to teddy bear lovers. Some of Australia's best-known authors have contributed their talents to very personalised and lovable teddy bears which are even more appealing through Denton's line and watercolour illustrations.
*Oxford University Press* 4–8 years ☆

### Tell Me A Tale: Stories, Songs And Things To Do
*Compiled and retold by Jean Chapman, illustrated by Kilmeny and Deborah Niland*
A collection of familiar stories suitable for preschool children in particular. Titles include: 'The Gingerbread Man', 'The Three Bears' and more contemporary stories . Poems and songs with musical scores are also included.
*Hodder & Stoughton* 3–8 years ☆

### The Puffin Children's Treasury
*Compiled by Clifton Fadiman*
Nursery rhymes, fables, myths, fairy and folktales are included along with a variety of poetry. Full-length picture books of classic status are reproduced, such as *Where The Wild Things Are, The Story About Ping* and *The Little Engine That Could*. For the older child, excerpts from long-time favourite novels are included.
*Viking Kestrel* 4–8 years

### Quirky Tails
*Paul Jennings*
This third collection of zany stories by Jennings is equally as appealing as the earlier ones. Magic, ghosts and all manner of unusual creatures are surprising and laughable. The language is particularly readable and attracts both reluctant and good readers.
*Puffin* 8–12 years ☆

## Badger On The Barge And Other Stories
*Janni Howker*
Five finely-crafted short stories set in England, and written by a very talented writer, all treat relationships between lonely young people and elderly strangers.
*Collins* 🅿 10 + years

## The Tall Book Of Tall Tales
*Jean Chapman, illustrated by Deborah Niland*
Tall tales are invariably exaggerated and often feature the most extravagant lies told with a strong dose of humour. An essential ingredient is exacting detail which makes the unbelievable real. Thirty-one tall tales appear here: five Australian and a sprinkling from other cultures. Line illustrations offer comical caricatures, perfect for these tales told with a storytelling quality.
*Hodder & Stoughton* 🅿 7–9 years ☆

## Mortimer's Cross
*Joan Aiken, illustrated by Quentin Blake*
In these three quirky, madcap short stories, Aiken successfully combines an adventuresome raven and his young owner Arabel, international gangsters, dinosaurs and pop stars in rollicking mysteries which seem entirely believable. Blake's illustrations add to the funny antics.
*Jonathan Cape* 🅷 8–10 years

## I Like This Story: A Taste Of Fifty Favourites
*Selected by Kaye Webb*
A collection of fifty excerpts from favourite novels is an excellent way to sample different genres such as fantasy, science fiction, realism and humour. Such novels as *Watership Down*, *The BFG* and *Charlotte's Web* demonstrate the wide-ranging styles, subjects and levels of sophistication included.
*Puffin* 🅿 9 + years

## The Big Dipper
*June Epstein et al, illustrated by Alison Lester*
Australian poems, stories, songs and activities included were produced by staff and students at the Institute of Early Childhood Development in Melbourne and illustrated with witty skill by Alison Lester. A thematic arrangement is a useful feature.
Also: *Big Dipper Rides Again; Big Dipper Returns*
*Oxford University Press* 🅿 3–7 years ☆

## Kissing The Toad And Other Stories By Young Australian Writers
*Doug MacLeod (ed)*
During the International Youth Year, 5000 young Australians entered their poetry and short stories in a competition. This collection includes twenty-three selections written by young people aged fourteen to twenty-five years. The raw power shown in style and content reflects such youthful concerns as racial prejudice, poverty, unemployment, drugs, disability and death.
*Penguin* 🅿 12 + years ☆

*Ratbags And Rascals*

# Traditional literature

These stories have been handed down orally for hundreds of years in all parts of the world. Their forms are varied: fables, folktales and fairytales for younger readers and listeners, and myths, legends, epics and sagas for older readers. These form a vast body of common stories known around the world. Fascinating cultural differences and similarities feature along with some of the most mesmerising tales and stunning illustrations in all of children's literature.

## Fables

### La Fontaine's Fables
*Jean de La Fontaine, translated by Diana Athill, illustrated by Romain Smith*
Unlike Aesop's well-known collections of fables, Frenchman Jean de La Fontaine's are in graceful verse. This handsome collection of thirty-one translated fables retains the lilt, rhythm and rhyme of the originals. The large page size and the beautiful illustrations make this an excellent collection to read aloud.
*Andre Deutsch* 🄷 7–10 years

### Aesop's Fables
*Retold by Michael Hague*
These thirteen fables featuring various animals which learn a moral lesson are perfect for Hague's talents. The animals are handsomely dressed and the settings have a warm, golden colouring. Such well-known morals as, 'Necessity is the mother of invention' and 'Look before you leap' are clearly and amusingly presented.
*Methuen* 🄷 6–10 years

### Once In A Wood
*Retold by Eve Rice*
Eve Rice, well-known picture book author and illustrator, has adapted ten familiar Aesop's fables into natural language patterns suitable for beginning readers. None of the flavour of the more complex language of Aesop is lost but the moral is made much clearer for young readers. Line illustrations and decorations on every page are excellent.
*Collins Lion* 🄿 6–9 years

### The North Wind And The Sun
*Jean de La Fontaine, illustrated by Brian Wildsmith*
The North Wind and the Sun each bet they can force a young man to remove his cloak. The brilliantly coloured illustrations show various events as the two forces pit their strengths.
*Oxford University Press* 🄿 7–9 years

### Three Rolls And One Doughnut
*Retold by Mirra Ginsburg, illustrated by Anita Lobel*
These brief Russian fables, folktales and riddles are witty and feature the usual assortment of rogues, wise men and tellers of tall tales. The simple language makes them suitable for developing readers and the illustrations, with their peasant clothing and amusing animals, are appealing.
*Longman Young* 🄷 7–10 years (Library)

## Folktales and fairytales

### Abbey Lubbers, Banshees And Boggarts
*Katharine Briggs, illustrated by Yvonne Gilbert*
Here is a fascinating insight into English fairies, their character, appearance and role in stories. For those who enjoy traditional literature, this book, arranged in dictionary format, is fascinating. Even short stories about many of these fairies are included. The seventy-one line illustrations are expertly detailed and coloured plates are sumptuous and suitably awesome.
*Kestrel* 🄷 9–15 years (Library)

### Aladdin
*Retold by Andrew Lang, illustrated by Errol Le Cain*
Aladdin, a poor tailor's son, inherits vast wealth through a bungling magician. A magical lantern and ring grant him his every wish and enable him to accumulate sufficient riches and a beautiful palace to win the hand of a princess. An evil magician gains the magical lantern and takes the princess and the castle with him to Africa. Aladdin's quick thinking brings this rich tale to a happy conclusion. Illustrations are remarkably decorative with ornate settings, wondrous costumes and striking full-page designs.
*Puffin* 🄿 7–9 years

## The Brothers Grimm

*Retold by Jacob and Wilhelm Grimm, translated by Brian Alderson, illustrated by Michael Foreman*
These thirty-one folktales newly translated have an excellent read-aloud quality and are close to the Grimm brothers' original collection. Illustrations include twenty-six watercolours, suitably romantic in mood, plus a number of black-and-white drawings. The large print and quality book design should attract readers.
*Gollancz* 🄷 9–12 years

## Folktales From Australia's Children Of The World

This collection of thirty-three folktales is drawn from ethnic groups in Australia. Original language versions with English translations are included from thirty non-English nationalities. Illustrations are in both black-and-white and colour.
*Ure Smith* 🄷 7–12 years (Library) ☆

## The Stone-Cutter: A Japanese Folk Tale

*Retold and illustrated by Gerald McDermott*
A lowly stonecutter aspires to be a wealthy prince and his wish is granted. Not satisfied, the stonecutter then wishes to be the sun, the cloud and finally a mountain. But he realises his lack of power when a lowly stonecutter chisels away at his surface. Beautifully stylised illustrations feature paper collage, simple strong shapes and bright colours.
*Puffin* 🄿 7–9 years

## Boastful Rabbit

*Retold by Ruth Manning-Sanders, illustrated by James Hodgson*
Each of these fifteen humorous stories from different countries features a rabbit in various misadventures. The language is simple and appropriate for the beginning reader as are the large type size and whimsical illustrations
*Methuen* 🄷 7–9 years (Library)

## Double Trouble: An Old Chinese Tale

*Retold by Jean Chapman, illustrated by Maya Winters*
Imagine a magical pot that doubles whatever is thrown inside. Riches and good fortune can be the result, but not when Mrs Huk-tuk accidentally falls inside and becomes double trouble for her husband. Suitably Chinese costumes and settings illustrated in a light-hearted style add to this humorous tale.
*Ashton Scholastic* 🄿 5–9 years ☆

## Rumpelstiltskin

*Retold and illustrated by Paul O Zelinsky*
Using a large format and lush, rich oil paintings, Zelinsky creates an unforgettable new version of this familiar Grimm tale. The illustrations are very effective in telling the story and creating memorable characters.
*Dutton* 🄷 7–10 years (Library)

## The Little Red Hen

*Margot Zemach*
A most appealing tale for young listeners, this story features a resourceful hen and her lazy friends, the goose, cat and pig. Zemach's illustrations perfectly capture personalities and give the story a warm, humorous touch.
*Puffin* 🄿 3–5 years

## The Faber Book Of Modern Fairy Tales

*Edited by Sara and Stephen Corrin, illustrated by Ann Strugnell*
Each of the fifteen stories featured draw from fairytales in theme, characters or style. Those included, though, are all twentieth century stories and represent some of the finest story makers. The stories' length and style make them excellent for reading aloud while the evocative line illustrations superbly reflect each story's mood.
*Faber & Faber* 🄿 9–12 years

**59**

## Favourite Fairy Tales Told In Greece

*Retold by Virginia Haviland, illustrated by Nonny Hogrogian*

Eight tales are included with language perfect for the developing reader. There are over a dozen books, all illustrated by well-known artists, in this series of fairytales from different countries.

*Little, Brown* **H** 7–9 years (Library)

## Stories From The Arabian Nights

*Retold by Naomi Lewis, illustrated by Anton Pieck*

Here are thirty of the 1001 stories recounted by Shahrazad to the King. These eastern tales are unlike many traditional ones — goodness is not always rewarded and justice is uncommon. Lewis's retellings are excellent and the delicate illustrations convey much of the culture.

*Methuen* **H** 9–12 years

## The Elves And The Shoemaker

*Retold by Jacob and Wilhelm Grimm, illustrated by Bernadette Watts*

A beautifully illustrated, favourite story about kindness and helping others in times of need. Two small men make shoes for a poor shoemaker until his luck returns. In gratitude, the shoemaker and his wife make clothing and shoes for the little men.

*North South* **H** 7–9 years

## Sleeping Beauty And Other Favourite Fairy Tales

*Charles Perrault and Madame de Beaumont, translated and compiled by Angela Carter, illustrated by Michael Foreman*

Ten of these twelve familiar tales are the versions collected by Frenchman Charles Perrault which feature alternate morals at the conclusion of each story. Two stories are Madame de Beaumont's versions which have greater character development. The familiar 'Cinderella', 'Little Red Riding Hood', 'Bluebeard' and 'Sleeping Beauty' are included  Strikingly intense watercolour illustrations throughout.

*Gollancz* **H** 8–10 years

## The Selfish Giant

*Oscar Wilde, illustrated by Lisbeth Zwerger*

A haunting, memorable story of Christian symbolism and fairytale appeal tells of a selfish giant who refuses to allow children to play in his garden and so is cursed with perpetual winter. One day, however, the children sneak in and bring spring with them. The giant sees a young boy unable to reach a tree and kindly places him there. In following years, the giant and children play until finally the small boy returns to take the giant to paradise. Illustrations in pale, delicate watercolours suit this gentle tale.

*Hutchinson* **H** 7–10 years

## Womenfolk And Fairy Tales

*Retold by Rosemary Minard, illustrated by Suzanna Klein*

Eight tales from cultures such as Celtic, European, Scandinavian, Japanese, Chinese and Persian are included. Each tale features heroines who exhibit qualities of intelligence, courage, ingenuity and initiative. Well-known collectors of tales and stories are represented in language of strong storytelling quality. Attractive illustrations.

*Houghton Mifflin* **H** 9–11 years

## The Story Of Chicken Licken

*Retold and illustrated by Jan Ormerod*

In this clever retelling, Chicken Licken is enacted as a school play with bold colouring and humorous dramatic flair. Below, in the audience, an adventuresome baby creates a diversion of her own.

*Walker* **P** 5–7 years ☆

## Kojuro And The Bears

*Adapted by Helen Smith, illustrated by . Junko Morimoto*

The philosophical theme of this Japanese folktale is that everything has its turn in life. And so Kojuro, a bear hunter, is ultimately killed by those he hunts and kills. Striking, haunting illustrations and a text rich in images make this a memorable, if complex, tale.

*Collins* **P** 7–10 years ☆

## Renard The Fox

*Rachel Anderson and David Bradby, illustrated by Bob Dewar*

These twelve stories starring the fox along with the wolf, crow and other animals have been adapted from a French collection of stories satirising society in medieval France. Incidents of cunning, treachery, and hypocrisy feature in these very funny stories. Witty watercolour illustrations and simple language and dialogue make these easy to read and perfect for storytelling.

*Oxford University Press* **H** 7–10 years

## A Piece Of Straw

*Adapted by Helen Smith, illustrated by Junko Morimoto*

Yohei, poor but kind, is rewarded for his good deeds with wealth and happiness. This familiar story is illustrated here as an unrolling scroll. Humour is presented in the predicaments and events of this Japanese tale and the text is beautiful to read aloud.

*Collins* **P** 6–9 years ☆

## Alan Garner's Book Of British Fairy Tales

*Retold by Alan Garner*

Garner retells twenty-one fairytales from all regions of Britain. The well-known 'Tom Tit Tot' and 'Molly Whuppy' are here, but many are less familiar. Each story is suitable for reading aloud or storytelling.

*Collins Lion* **P** 9–12 years

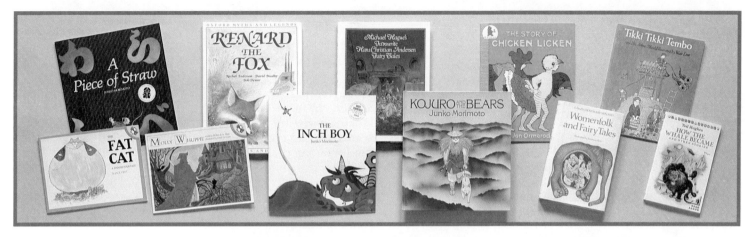

## The Fat Cat
*Translated by Jack Kent*
This Danish folktale features a greedy cat who first eats the gruel then its pot and one after the other a host of unwary people. He continues to eat until he meets the woodcutter who cuts the cat open and frees all his victims. A final illustration shows the woodcutter administering to a rather thin cat with tape plastered over the offending hole.
*Puffin* **P** 7–9 years

## Clever Gretchen And Other Forgotten Folk Tales
*Retold by Alison Lurie, illustrated by Margot Tomes*
Like other feminist folktales, these fifteen stories feature women who are active, witty, brave and resourceful, and able to overcome dangers where needed. A brief note gives each tale's origin. Very appealing illustrations.
*Heinemann* **H** 9–12 years

## How The Whale Became And Other Stories
*Ted Hughes*
Eleven brief tales relate how animals assumed their present forms or behaviour. Each is told with rich language that rolls easily off the tongue and is a storytelling or read-aloud delight. Stories feature the whale, fox, hyena, tortoise, bee, cat and others.
*Puffin* **P** 7–10 years

## Michael Hague's Favourite Hans Christian Andersen Fairy Tales
*Hans Christian Andersen*
Andersen is the world's most prolific and well-known writer of fairytales. Hague has selected nine to illustrate including the familiar, 'The Snow Queen', 'Thumbelina', 'The Little Match Girl', 'The Ugly Duckling' and 'The Little Mermaid'. These poignant tales haunt the imagination and Hague's illustrations are a perfect accompaniment.
*Methuen* **H** 6–10 years

## The Inch Boy
*Adapted by Helen Smith, illustrated by Junko Morimoto*
Despite his diminutive size, Issunboshi, the inch boy, dreams of becoming a Samurai and serving the noble lord in Kyoto. This daring, adventurous Japanese tale is beautifully told in rich prose and illustrated in bold, stylised fashion.
*Collins* **P** 6–9 years ☆

## Molly Whuppie
*Retold by Walter de la Mare, illustrated by Errol Le Cain*
A much-favoured Spanish tale is beautifully retold by the author and illustrated in glowing, ornately detailed paintings. Resourceful and clever Molly Whuppie outwits a giant and gains princes for her sisters. The giant is suitably frightening and his repeated refrain when outsmarted adds to the read-aloud pleasure
*Puffin* **P** 7–9 years

## Tikki Tikki Tembo
*Retold by Arlene Mosel, illustrated by Blair Lent*
This amusing story gives one version why the Chinese give their first born sons short names. Long ago a first-born son was named Tikki tikki tembo-no sa rembo-chari bari ruchi-pip peri pembo and almost drowned as a result. The repeated name, rhythmic and patterned phrases, plus illustrations with a Chinese flavour make this a favourite.
*Scholastic* **P** 7–9 years

## The Knee-High Man And Other Tales
*Retold by Julius Lester, illustrated by Ralph Pinto*
Lester has made a major contribution to American black literature. These six brief animal tales will be enjoyed by beginning readers. Some stories tell of cunning and trickery and others explain why dogs hate cats. Each is amusing and highly readable
*Dial* **P** 7–9 years

### The People Could Fly
*Retold by Virginia Hamilton, illustrated by Leo and Diane Dillon*
Lively animal trickster tales, ghost and devil stories, fantasies and narratives of slaves feature in this handsome collection. Illustrations in grey watercolour wash are oustanding and the typeface and paper quality make this a sumptuous book.
*Walker* 🇭 9–12 years

### The Seal Mother
*Retold and illustrated by Mordicai Gerstein*
Each Midsummer's Eve, the longest night of the year, the seals in the North Atlantic take human form to sing and dance. Once a fisherman witnesses this event, falls in love with a beautiful seal and steals her sealskin so she must remain forever human.
*Methuen* 🇭 7–9 years

### Red Fairybook
*Compiled by Andrew Lang, Brian Alderson (ed), illustrated by Faith Jaques*
Andrew Lang's series of various coloured fairytale collections began in 1889 with the *Blue Fairybook*. Many others followed and several of these have been reprinted with small textual changes and new illustrations. These thirty-three tales came from such countries as Russia, Germany, England and Scandinavia.
*Dover* 🅿 10–12 years

### The Juniper Tree And Other Tales From Grimm
*Retold by Jacob and Wilhelm Grimm, translated by Lore Segal and Randall Jarrell, illustrated by Maurice Sendak*
Twenty-seven tales collected by the Grimm brothers are newly translated and given special prominence with Sendak's fine illustrations. Familiar tales such as 'Snow White' and 'Hansel and Gretel' are included, but the emphasis is on the more mysterious and awesome of the Grimm tales. Sendak's illustrations enhance and extend this mood, making this collection suitable for older fans of the German folktales.
*Bodley Head* 🇭 9–12 years (Library)

### The Devil With The Three Golden Hairs
*Retold by Jacob and Wilhelm Grimm, illustrated by Nonny Hogrogian*
In this Grimm brothers' tale, a young boy marries a princess despite the King's efforts to have him killed. In desperation, the King insists he may not keep his bride unless he obtains three hairs from the devil's head. This the young boy does. His courage and cunning give him a clever ploy to send the king away. Illustrations are soft and delicately coloured.
*Knopf* 🇭 8–10 years

# Modern imitators

**Modern imitators poke fun at some of these traditional stories: twisting plots, transforming characters, modernising dialogue and adding zany illustrations.**

### Revolting Rhymes
*Roald Dahl, illustrated by Quentin Blake*
The familiar Cinderella and Little Red Riding Hood were never like these characters. Little Red Riding Hood carries a pistol in her knickers and the prince chops off the heads of Cinderella's ugly sisters. Roald Dahl's black humour has great appeal, especially when coupled with Quentin Blake's equally amusing illustrations.
*Puffin* 🅿 7–12 years

### Princess Smartypants
*Babette Cole*
Princess Smartypants enjoys being a Ms and detests the idea of marriage. When pressed by her parents into seeking a suitor, she sets impossible tasks for would-be suitors. None succeed until Prince Swashbuckle arrives. So pleased is the Princess with his achievements that she bestows a magical kiss and the Prince becomes a warty toad! Hilarious illustrations extend the text which reveals only the bare story.
*Collins Lion* 🅿 7–10 years

### Foxy Fables
*Tony Ross*
An operatic crow, a fox in love with a cat and a stork that outwits a fox are just a few of the humorous characters in these stories which are clever parodies of the fables. Those knowledgeable will recognise the hare and the tortoise fable, but what a difference! The illustrations match these zany tales by a master of humour.
*Puffin* 🅿 8–10 years

### Jeremiah In The Dark Woods
*Allan Ahlberg*
Jeremiah Obadiah Jackenory Jones lives with his grandmother in the dark woods. When Jeremiah attempts to deliver jam tarts to his aunt, he encounters a number of familiar nursery rhyme and fairytale characters who add to the adventure.
*Viking Kestrel* 🅿 7–9 years

### The Jolly Postman Or Other People's Letters
*Janet and Allan Ahlberg*
An inspired fairytale parody with a parade of well-known nursery characters. A postman delivers letters to giants, witches, a wolf, Cinderella and others and the reader is invited to read these letters which refer to familiar characters. Jokes abound here and the illustrations and text will have all who are familiar with the original tales in hysterics. Many details invite repeated re-readings.
*Heinemann* 🇭 7–12 years

## Brock And The Dragon
*Robin Klein, illustrated by Rodney McRae*
Here's a knight who prefers lute playing to rescuing damsels in distress, a beautiful princess resourceful and strong and a dragon who hates the tradition of devouring female sacrifices. These ingredients make a very clever send-up of the traditional prince-rescues-princess tale.
*Hodder & Stoughton* **P**
6–8 years ☆

## Jim And The Beanstalk
*Raymond Briggs*
Jim's trip up the beanstalk takes him to a rather elderly giant — the son of the giant met by Jack. This giant has no teeth, poor eyes and no hair. The giant requests false teeth, eye glasses and a wig, then finds his appetite returns causing Jim to quickly retreat down the beanstalk. The giant drops down a thankyou note and a gold coin in gratitude.
*Puffin* **P** 5–9 years

## Snow White In New York
*Fiona French*
Placing Snow White in a contemporary urban setting reinforces this traditional tale as a universal one of jealousy, love and intrigue. Snow White's stepmother appears as the Queen of the Underworld, determined to rid herself of her stepdaughter. Illustrations are outstanding.
*Oxford University Press* **H**
7–12 years

## Badjelly The Witch
*Spike Milligan*
In this funny spoof on fairytales, there is an unusual assortment of characters: tin lions, worms, eagles, giants and witches. When two children lose their cow, they go in pursuit but get lost in dark woods and meet the 'baddest' witch in the world. The text is hand lettered and decorated with humorous illustrations.
*W H Allen* **P** 8–10 years

## The Practical Princess And Other Liberating Fairy Tales
*Jay Williams, illustrated by Rick Schreiter*
Six light-hearted send-ups of familiar fairytales will have readers laughing. Here princesses do not wait to be rescued, princes are bumbling and dragons gullible.
Black silhouette illustrations highlight characters and incidents.
*Scholastic* **P** 8–12 years

## Petronella
*Jay Williams*
When Princess Petronella comes of age, she goes out into the world to find a prince. Because she is brave, kind and talented, she succeeds at three dangerous and difficult tasks. The twists of plot which alter the expected are very humorous and the strong heroine has great appeal.
*Parents' Magazine* **H**
7–10 years (Library)

## Little Red Riding Hood
*Retold by Tony Ross*
In this version, Granny is a scatty old woman to whom Red Riding Hood takes stout and tarts. Not unexpectedly, she meets the wolf who gobbles down both her and Granny. The woodcutter knocks the wolf on the head, turns him upside down and out pops Granny and granddaughter, 'angry and sticky' but unhurt. The wolf gives up eating people and tries to grow vegetables instead.
*Puffin* **P** 7–10 years

## Fables
*Arnold Lobel*
These twenty highly amusing tales use the traditional fable format but cleverly introduce some interesting twists. Rather unexpected morals are added and the illustrations, imaginative and humorous, have great appeal.
*Macmillan* **P** 7–10 years

# Myths, legends, epics and sagas

## Why Mosquitoes Buzz In People's Ears
*Retold by Verna Aardema, illustrated by Leo and Diane Dillon*
A mosquito annoys an iguana and this triggers off a series of events which end in the accidental death of a baby owl. The sad mother refuses to wake the sun and so the jungle remains in darkness. A meeting of all the animals unravels the events and results in the mosquito's punishment. Beautiful illustrations in watercolours, pastels and Indian ink are striking and very effective for this African legend.
*Dial* **P** 6–9 years

## Saint George And The Dragon
*Retold by Margaret Hodges, illustrated by Trina Schart Hyman*
The Red Cross Knight is sent by the Queen of the Fairies to destroy a deadly dragon which is terrorising the land. He is accompanied by Una, a princess who is determined to help in the dragon's destruction. Illustrations are bordered with intricate designs.
*Little, Brown* **H** 7–10 years

## The God Beneath The Sea
*Leon Garfield and Edward Blishen, illustrated by Charles Keeping*
In this amazing retelling of the Greek myths, the authors have developed the myths into a continuous story. There is a strong sense of continuity and greater logic here than in many other standard sources.
*Corgi* **H** 10–15 years (Library)

## Djugurba: Tales From The Spirit Time
*N Maralngura et al*
Aborigines training to be teachers have retold and illustrated these fourteen traditional stories from various areas of Australia. This book is the first in which Aborigines retell their own stories. A simple style and bold, striking illustrations feature in these creation tales.
*University Press* **H** 7–10 years ☆

## The Gift Of The Sacred Dog
*Retold by Paul Goble*
This legend of the Indians of the North American Great Plains relates the coming of the horse. A young Indian boy despairs when his tribe is unable to find buffalo for food and seeks the help of the Great Spirit. The horse, called the Sacred Dog, is the gift of the Great Spirit. The illustrations are dramatic and evoke the Indian culture.
*Bradbury* **H** 7–9 years (Library)

## Norse Gods And Giants
*Ingri and Edgar Parin d'Aulaire*
This collection of Norse mythology remains one of the most attractive ones for children. Here the reader meets the god Odin, ruler of the other gods and humans, Thor and his mighty hammer and others. The endpapers outline the nine Norse worlds and the frontispiece identifies the major gods. Throughout the illustrations capture the force and vigour of these ancient tales.
*Doubleday* **P** 9–12 years

## The Clown Of God
*Retold by Tomie de Paola*
A poignant Italian legend about a once famous juggler now old and jeered is retold and illustrated in a medieval style, the period of the tale's origin. In a final performance before the Madonna and Child, Giovanni gives his most spectacular juggling act and a miracle occurs. The setting is beautifully rendered and the tale has much pathos.
*Magnet* **P** 7–9 years

## Sinabouda Lily
*Robin Anderson*
In this Papua New Guinean legend, little Sinabouda Lily is captured by a wicked witch who is punished by being turned into stone. The bold, stylised illustrations reflect a lush tropical vegetation and have great appeal.
*Oxford University Press* **H** 6–9 years (Library)

## When The Snake Bites The Sun
*Retold by Pamela Lofts*
There are several legends in this series based on Aboriginal tales from Western Australia. The striking illustrations are adapted from those by Aboriginal children. Each legend explains a natural phenomenon or an animal's creation. This tale explains the beginning and importance of day and night.
Also: *How The Birds Got Their Colours; Echidna And The Shade Tree; Dunbi The Owl; The Bat And The Crocodile*
*Ashton Scholastic* **P** 6–9 years ☆

## Fabled Cities, Princes And Jinn
*Retold by Khairat Al-Saleh, illustrated by Rashad N Salim and Peter Dennis*
These myths and legends are divided into two sections: pre-Islam Arabia and the Golden Age of the Arab Muslim world. Each tale is brief and accompanied by both line illustrations and handsome decorative paintings which emphasise the symbols of Arab myths and legends. An introductory section on the Arab world sets the context for the stories. Other useful inclusions are a guide to pronunciation and symbols, sources of stories and an index.
*Hodder & Stoughton* **H** 9–12 years

### Turramulli The Giant Quinkin
*Percy Trezise and*
*Dick Roughsey*
Together, these two men, one an Aborigine, have retold and illustrated the traditional stories of the Cape York peninsula. This tale concerns two children pursued by the evil Quinkin but saved by the good Timara creatures. The landscapes are superb and the stories strong. Much of the Aboriginal culture is revealed in this set of ten stories.
*Collins* **P** 7–9 years ☆

### Tales Of King Arthur
*Retold by James Riordan,*
*illustrated by Victor Ambrus*
Drawing on various printed versions of England's King Arthur legend, Riordan tells twelve stories beginning with one which sets the historical content. Illustrations are lusty and bold, and costuming and settings evoke the era.
*Hodder & Stoughton* **H**
10–12 years

### Gods, Men And Monsters From The Greek Myths
*Retold by Michael Gibson,*
*illustrated by*
*Giovanni Caselli*
Twenty-six familiar Greek myths are included together with a useful family tree and map to identify the site of various stories. Here are the tales of Apollo, Pan, Hercules, Perseus, Psyche, Eurydice and others with paintings and line illustrations.
*Hodder & Stoughton* **H**
10–15 years

### The Saga Of Erik The Viking
*Retold by Terry Jones,*
*illustrated by*
*Michael Foreman*
These twenty exciting stories, retold from the Nordic sagas, about Erik, a Viking warrior, link together with common characters. Watercolour illustrations in an imaginative style capture the dangers, and tense action
*Puffin* **P** 10–12 years

### Robin Hood: His Life And Legend
*Retold by Bernard Miles,*
*illustrated by Victor Ambrus*
In these fifteen tales, Miles retells Robin Hood's exploits featuring Little John, Maid Marian, Friar Tuck and others. Each tale is in contemporary language but the dialogue is mildly flavoured to recapture the period. The boldly coloured, expertly costumed illustrations add appeal.
*Hodder & Stoughton* **H**
10–12 years

### Seasons Of Splendour
*Retold by Madhur Jaffrey,*
*illustrated by Michael Foreman*
These beautifully retold myths and folktales of India reveal a rich source of stories about gods and goddesses, royalty and demons of Hindu epics. Each is retold in crisp, smooth language and Foreman's watercolour illustrations are suitably horrific or romantic.
*Hodder & Stoughton* **H**
8–12 years

### The Loon's Necklace
*Retold by William Toye,*
*illustrated by Elizabeth Cleaver*
According to the Canadian Tsimshian Indian legend, a loon (waterbird) gives an old man his sight and in gratitude, the elderly man gives the loon his treasured shell necklace. Thereafter, the loon has a white collar and speckles on his back. The collage and linocuts in bold colours offer a stark strength to this beautiful tale.
*Oxford University Press* **H**
7–9 years

### Beowulf
*Retold by Kevin Crossley-Holland, illustrated by Charles Keeping*
Beowulf is probably the best-known Norse epic. This version, retold in rich prose of strong imagery, features the warrior Beowulf's three battles against evil. These are highlighted by the illustrator's sombre, stark, line drawings.
*Oxford University Press* **H**
10–15 years

# Fantasy and science fiction

Many of these stories prove that sometimes the oldest are the best. Escape into an imaginary, often exhilarating, world unlike our ordinary one, full of believable heroes and heroines who overcome great dangers and accomplish enviable feats. Haunting and memorable, these books are perfect for sharing.

## Imaginary lands and heroic adventures

### Alice's Adventures In Wonderland
*Lewis Carroll*
*illustrated by John Tenniel*
Many adults recall Alice as one of their most memorable childhood books. Word puns, parodies and allusions to the wider world make this a multi-layered book.
*Macmillan* **H** 10 + years

### Freaky Friday
*Mary Rodgers*
Annabel Andrews, awakens one morning to experience the most bizarre day of her life — in her mother's body but with her own personality. Hilarity characterises the day as Annabel tries to cope and gains sympathy for mothers.
*Puffin* **P** 9–12 years

### The Story Of Peter Pan
*J M Barrie, illustrated by Mabel Lucie Atwell*
All the elements of a spellbinding story are here. Peter Pan comes from Neverland and takes Wendy Darling and her brothers back to his world. Numerous adventures and battles occur and the pace of the plot never slows. While some parts seem old-fashioned and sentimental by today's standards, the idea of a magical land inhabited by children who are forever young retains its appeal.
*Hodder & Stoughton* **H**
7–10 years

### Tuck Everlasting
*Natalie Babbitt*
A thought-provoking fantasy about the consequences of immortality. The Tuck family drink spring water in their woodland home and unwittingly find they never age nor can they be hurt. Eloquent prose, strong characterisation and a tightly knit plot make this novel outstanding.
*Collins* **P** 10–13 years

### Space Demons
*Gillian Rubinstein*
'Space Demons' is a highly sophisticated computer game which physically ensnares its players, exploiting and manipulating their emotions. As the space demons intrude upon the outside world, the youthful players draw together to defeat their purpose. Relentless action and absorbing themes combine in this taut science fiction novel.
*Omnibus* **P** 10–13 years ☆

### Dark Is Rising
(series title)
*Susan Cooper*
These five novels treat the age-old theme of good and evil. Three ordinary children work with young Will Stanton, recently joined with the forces of good, to maintain the balance of power. Time travels back to King Arthur's period and forward to the future. Evil creatures and suspenseful battles draw readers to this series. The characterisation is slightly uneven and not all of the five novels are equal in quality, but overall this series has a loyal following.
Titles in reading order: *Over Sea, Under Stone; The Dark Is Rising; Greenwitch; The Grey King; Silver On The Tree*
*Puffin* **P** 10 + years

### Dragonsong
*Anne McCaffrey*
Menolly lives on the planet Pern where huge, flying dragons guard against the deadly spores which destroy all living matter. Against this exciting setting, Menolly fights to achieve her dream of becoming a harpist, an unsuitable undertaking for a female according to her father. When Menolly teaches fire lizards to sing, she gains some acceptance. In this exciting trilogy called *Harper Hall*, McCaffrey explores the role of women and themes of rebellion and alienation.
Sequels in reading order: *Dragondrums; Dragonsinger*
*Corgi* **P** 10 + years

## The Borrowers
*Mary Norton*
The borrowers are like humans in every respect but only one-twelfth their size. Naturally, life is full of dangers and adventures for such people who 'borrow' objects from the larger world to make their home. Throughout the series, the Clock family, Arrietty and her parents, Pod and Homily, search for security and a home. Their greatest threats come from humans who attempt to capture and exhibit them, but owls and cats are equally dangerous. Humour, suspense and believable detail together with the freedom-loving Arrietty and her friend Spiller make these appealing to read aloud.
Titles in reading order: *The Borrowers Afield; The Borrowers Afloat; The Borrowers Aloft; Poor Stainless; The Borrowers Avenged*
*Puffin* 🅿 10–12 years

## Chronicles Of Narnia
(series title)
*C S Lewis*
A deeply satisfying fantasy filling seven volumes. Christian symbolism lies beneath the many adventurous battles to save the magical land of Narnia from evil rulers. Aslan, a powerful all-knowing lion (and Christ figure), features in many battles as do the four children, Edmund, Lucy, Peter and Eustace. Central to the plots are such philosophical concepts as looking beyond immediate rewards, giving obedience to a higher good, and being true to oneself. Beautifully detailed, exciting plots, and characters worth caring about have made these one of the most popular children's fantasies ever.
Titles in reading order: *The Magician's Nephew; The Lion, The Witch And The Wardrobe; The Horse And His Boy; The Last Battle*
*Collins Lion* 🅿 9 + years

## Chronicles Of Prydain
(series title)
*Lloyd Alexander*
These five novels comprise one of the best contemporary fantasies. Based on the Welsh Mabinogion legend, they relate the adventures of Taran, an orphan, who through heroic deeds achieves a strong identity. Elements of magic, humour and warmth appear. Titles in reading order: *The Book Of Three; The Black Cauldron; The Castle Of Llyr; Taran Wanderer; The High King*
*Collins* 🅿 10 + years

## The Hero And The Crown
*Robin McKinley*
Like the earlier related novel, *The Blue Sword,* this one deals with fantasy's traditional battle of good and evil and the adolescent quest for identity. Aerin is a forceful, believable heroine; the plot is intricately developed and the setting memorable.
*Futura* 🅿 10 + years

## Master Of The Grove
*Victor Kelleher*
Despite his memory loss, fourteen-year-old Derin feels compelled to follow the awesome Marna of the Witch people on a dangerous quest to rescue his avowed father. In this gripping fantasy, the reader stumbles through a complex maze of innuendoes which climax in a surprising, well-crafted conclusion.
*Penguin* 🅿 10 + years ☆

## The Once And Future King
*T H White*
This classic fantasy follows the legend of King Arthur from childhood to the tragic fall of his court. Superb storytelling brings Arthur's carefree childhood and his trouble-filled years as king to life. A powerful, descriptive style, astute pacing and well-rounded characters evoke all the emotions and make this a superb novel.
*Puffin* 🅿 10 + years

**67**

### Finn Family Moomintroll
*Tove Jansson*
The Moomins are gentle, happy and friendly creatures descended from trolls but looking rather like hippopotamuses. Though imaginary, the Moomins resemble humans, especially in their strong sense of responsibility to one another. An amusing cast of highly imaginative characters parade through these warm adventures inevitably arising from the Moomins' curious natures. Illustrations by the author add to these enjoyable tales.
Also: *The Happy Moomins; Moominsummer Madness*
*Puffin* 🅿 9–11 years

### The Hobbit
*J R R Tolkien*
Bilbo Baggins is an unassuming, home-loving hobbit, living underground and enjoying a peaceful, uneventful life. Then Gandalf a wizard arrives and announces Bilbo is to accompany twelve dwarfs on a mission to retrieve their ancestors' treasure from Smaug, an evil dragon. Bilbo proves heroic in his many battles with slimy creatures, wild wolves, goblins, spiders and other frightening creatures. Intricately detailed plot and setting and a memorable hero transport the reader into a magical, unforgettable world.
Also: *Lord Of The Rings*
*Allen & Unwin* 🅿 10 + years

# Tales of magic, myths and spirits

### The Book Of Wirrun
(series title)
*Patricia Wrightson*
Wirrun is a young Aborigine sought by Ko-in, a spirit of the Australian landscape, to restore harmony to the land. In this trilogy, Wirrun is a reluctant but brave hero. During the quests he must undertake, he is hindered and helped by the Australian spirit creatures to achieve a self-identity, find human and spiritual love and discover true friendship. Poetic prose and a slow-paced plot demand a mature reader but the novels are a masterful achievement and will be long-remembered. Titles in reading order: *The Ice Is Coming; The Dark Bright Water; Behind The Wind*
*Puffin* 🅿 11 + years ☆

### The Nimbin
*Jenny Wagner, illustrated by Inga Moore*
Philippa experiences a summer holiday like none other when she is adopted by the strange little nimbin. A creature which is vulnerable and appealing but exhibits an iron will, a nasty temper, and a huge appetite for sweets causes Philippa no end of trouble while she helps it return home.
*Puffin* 🅿 8–11 years ☆

### The Ghost Of Thomas Kempe
*Penelope Lively*
Young James Harrison has a curious and accident-prone nature, so when strange signs and events occur he is blamed. But the fault is Thomas Kempe's, a ghost from the seventeenth century, who wishes to practise his sorcery arts once again with James as his apprentice. Many bizarre, startling and humorous events occur before James is able to convince the ghost to return to his grave. Well-plotted and lively from beginning to end.
*Puffin* 🅿 10–12 years

### Pippi Longstocking
*Astrid Lindgren, illustrated by Richard Kennedy*
Pippi is a long-standing favourite heroine created by a Swedish author. Conveniently without parents to direct her behaviour and bestowed with superhuman strength and a mischievous wit, Pippi engages in outrageous exploits. Pippi aspires to be a pirate and being a 'young lady' holds no attraction whatsoever. Understandably, such a theme, coupled with an enviable carrot-topped lass, makes for enjoyable, light reading.
Also: *Pippi Goes Abroad; Pippi In The South Seas; Pippi On The Run*
*Puffin* 🅿 8–10 years

### Matilda
*Roald Dahl, illustrated by Quentin Blake*
Matilda is no ordinary five-year-old in this modern fairytale. She is bright and brave. However, she is lumbered with uncaring parents and put upon by her dreadful headmistress, Miss Trunchbull. But then there's lovely Miss Honey, Matilda's sweet (naturally) kindergarten teacher who balances the image of the thoroughly bad headmistress. How Matilda defeats Miss Trunchbull is the plot and Dahl gives readers his usual exaggerated and humorous dose of gore, violence and slapstick humour. Blake's illustrations are suitably quirky and expressive of the calamities throughout.
*Bodley Head* 🅷 9–12 years

### My Sister Sif
*Ruth Park*
Rikoriko is half-human, half-seacreature. Her mother is a mermaid; her brother Stig lives with the seacreatures. Both Rikoriko and her sister Sif, who attend school in Sydney, must return to their home in the Pacific as Sif suffers in the city environment. The story relates the escape back home and the effect of a scientist's visit on their family. A major underlying theme is the pollution of the world's oceans.
*Puffin* 🅿 10 + years ☆

### The BFG
*Roald Dahl, illustrated by Quentin Blake*
A Big Friendly Giant (BFG) and a resourceful orphan girl save the world from nine nasty giants who gobble humans. What are 'whizzpoppers', 'icky poos' and 'cattlepiddlers'? Finding out leaves the reader laughing from page one to the grand finale. Irresistible reading and a firm favourite with children.
*Puffin* P 9–12 years

### The Haunting
*Margaret Mahy*
Barnaby is only eight and desperately frightened by ghostly hauntings initiated by his great-uncle Cole. There is a wonderfully complex mystery which is slowly unravelled, teasing the reader all the while. Strong visual language gives this book its own frightening atmosphere and readers should be prepared to be scared!
*Magnet* P 11 + years

### The Nargun And The Stars
*Patricia Wrightson*
Young Simon Brent, an orphan, joins relatives on a large Australian sheep station. But there are ancient Aboriginal creatures who have long inhabited the land: the trickster Potkoorok; the Turongs, tree spirits; the Nyols, cave dwellers; and an ancient, awesome rock, the Nargun. The Nargun's movements and relentless destruction of the property are both chilling and exciting. Simon's heroic battle to save his relatives and the property is breathtaking reading and the descriptive passages are particularly moving read aloud.
*Puffin* P 10–12 years ☆

### The Children Of Green Knowe
*Lucy M Boston, illustrated by Peter Boston*
Sensitively written, this is the first of five stories centring on a haunted medieval manor. In this story, Tolly visits his great-grandmother, Mrs Oldknow, and meets three children, ghosts from the seventeenth century. There is a gentle, melancholy mood about these stories and the style is haunting.
*Puffin* P 10–12 years

### Mary Poppins
*P L Travers*
Mary Poppins, a prim, British nanny, arrives magically on the wind to care for the four Banks children. Surrounding her is a magic that turns the world upside down; her rewards and punishments are fair but highly unusual. She will leave, she reveals, when the wind changes. Meanwhile, this nanny is entertaining, amusing and like no other.
*Puffin* P 9–11 years

### A Little Fear
*Patricia Wrightson*
Mrs Tucker prefers to live in a cottage with only her dog for company than to go to a home for the elderly. But an ancient land spirit, the Njimbin, already claims ownership. Ferocious battles continue until the Njimbin evokes the swarming natural life to instil a little fear into his enemy.
*Puffin* P 9–11 years ☆

### The Witches
*Roald Dahl, illustrated by Quentin Blake*
When a Norwegian grandmother teaches her grandson how to recognise witches, who would believe he would witness the annual convention of witches and hear their plan to turn England's children into mice? The witches' plans are cleverly foiled by the humans' quick thinking and daring. Funny, exciting, believable — a compelling read throughout.
*Puffin* P 9–12 years

### House With A Clock In Its Walls
*John Bellairs, illustrated by Edward Gorey*
Imagine a clock hidden within walls which is programmed to end the world! This crisis is faced by Lewis, a ten-year-old orphan, who lives with his Warlock Uncle Jonathan, a practitioner of white magic. Together they and Mrs Zimmerman, a neighbour witch, search for the clock. Suitably scary illustrations. Also: *The Figure In The Shadows; The Letter, The Witch, And The Ring*
*Dial* **P** 9–12 years

### A Stranger Came Ashore
*Mollie Hunter*
One stormy night, Finn Learson appears from the wild waters off the Shetland Islands. Is he who he claims to be or is he, as twelve-year-old Rob believes, a legendary Great Selkie, capable of shedding his seal skin, taking on human appearance and capturing young maidens for his sea kingdom? Rob's grandfather has warned him of grave dangers, but no one listens except for an inscrutable wizard. Magic of land and sea come together in a fierce battle.
*Collins Lion* **P** 10 + years

# Talking toys and animals

### The Indian In The Cupboard
*Lynne Reid Banks, illustrated by Robin Jacques*
An imaginative and lively fantasy about toys which come to life. Omri receives a little plastic Indian, seven centimetres high, to add to his collection. But when placed in an old wall cupboard Little Bear the Indian comes to life. Adding to this absorbing story is a tiny toy cowboy, Boone, who also comes to life. These miniature people are very real and the relationships between them and the boys have great appeal.
Sequel: *The Return Of The Indian*
*Collins Lion* **P** 9–12 years

### The Adventures Of Pinocchio
*Carlo Collodi (pseudonym of Carlo Lorenzini)*
Gepetto, a woodcarver, receives little thanks from the little puppet boy, Pinocchio, he has lovingly created. As soon as he is able, Pinocchio runs away and is led astray. Pinocchio at last chooses the love of Gepetto over a life of mischief and idleness. A fast-paced, boisterous series of adventures starring a naughty youth — this classic has never lost its appeal.
*Macmillan* **H** 9–11 years (Library)

### The Mousewife
*Rumer Godden, illustrated by William Pene du Bois*
In this whimsical, gentle fantasy a dissatisfied mousewife yearns for something more in life. An imprisoned dove fills the mousewife's head with tales of flying and a beautiful earth. One night, the mousewife frees the dove to restore her happiness. Line and grey wash illustrations suit the mood.
*Viking* **H** 8–10 years

### The Velveteen Rabbit
*Margery Williams, illustrated by Michael Hague*
At one time the velveteen rabbit was beautiful and new. But when he is forgotten by his owner, he is snubbed by the other toys. A 'real' toy is one loved by a child over a long time. A sentimental story of love, friendship and loyalty given much character and appeal by the illustrations.
*Heinemann* **H** 6–9 years

### Mrs. Frisby And The Rats Of NIMH
*Robert O'Brien*
Mrs Frisby seeks help with her seriously ill son and discovers a super-intelligent society of rats who can read, write and much more. In this exciting animal fantasy of an unusual life style, O'Brien makes subtle comments on animal experimentation. However, this does not get in the way of a moving adventure story of danger and survival.
*Puffin* **P** 10–12 years

### Abel's Island
*William Steig*
Abel and Amanda, a loving and devoted mouse couple, are married but a year when a violent hurricane carries Abel away to an island. For a full year, Abel survives despite a viciously cold winter and a watchful owl which swoops noiselessly on her prey. Abel's thoughts of Amanda give him hope and he reassesses his thoughts about life, friends and loved ones. A moving story of courage and endurance with intricate details of life on the island. Illustrations throughout are perfect.
*Collins Lion* **P** 9–12 years

### The Mouse And His Child
*Russell Hoban, illustrated by Lillian Hoban*
A pair of mechanical dancing mice, father and son, are bought one Christmas and separated from their companions in a toyshop. Broken, then discarded on a rubbish dump, the pair are wound up by a passing tramp and thus begins their pursuit of love, security and a home. Relentlessly pursued by Manny the rat, cruel ruler of the dump, the two mice brave many ordeals before achieving happiness. Moving and suspenseful, the story never loses interest and both surface and underlying meanings make this a novel for all ages.
*Puffin* **P** 10 + years

### The Mouse And The Motorcycle
*Beverly Cleary, illustrated by Louis Darling*
Ralph, an adventurous young mouse, lives in a mousehole at the Mountain View Inn. When Keith and his parents stay at the inn, Ralph takes a fancy to the boy's toy motorcycle which is just his size. The exploits of Ralph and the friendship between him and Keith offer much warmth and humour in an easy-to-read, fast-paced fantasy.
*Puffin* **P** 8–10 years

### The Magic Pudding
*Norman Lindsay*
The adventures of Bunyip Bluegum and his friends, owner and eaters of Albert the magic pudding, make hilarious reading. The language, peppered with songs, verse and rich insults is a read-aloud delight. Lindsay's illustrations are masterly.
*Angus & Robertson* **P**
8–12 years ☆

### Charlotte's Web
*E B White, illustrated by Garth Williams*
Wilbur the pig is bound for Christmas slaughtering until his clever friend Charlotte the spider spins in her web such words as, 'Some pig' and 'terrific'. Though Charlotte dies at the story's end, the sad event is tempered by Wilbur's rescue of her egg sac. A memorable story with equally appealing illustrations.
*Puffin* **P** 9–12 years

### The Cricket In Times Square
*George Selden*
New York's Times Square will never be the same after the arrival of Chester the Cricket, a concert musician. He and Mario, whose parents run a newsstand, become friends. Tucker Mouse and Harry Cat, along with Chester, amusingly boost the troubled newsstand business. Warm-hearted and amusing illustrations.
*Puffin* **P** 9–12 years

### The Wind In The Willows
*Kenneth Grahame, illustrated by E H Shepard*
In this long-favoured, beautifully written fantasy, home and security are important pursuits for Mole, River Rat and Badger. Toad, on the other hand, is wayward, conceited and obsessed by motor cars and adventures in the wider world. Their lives intertwine in a series of skirmishes and events. After a frightening battle with weasels and stoats for the possession of Toad Hall, the four friends settle into a peaceful and happy existence. Best read aloud in the younger years and preferably using a well-illustrated edition.
*Magnet* **P** 10 + years

### Watership Down
*Richard Adams*
In this long, intricately detailed and memorable fantasy, a warren of rabbits search for a new home as their own is to be destroyed by land developers. Their quest leads them through numerous dangers and threatening societies, one a cruel dictatorship, another seemingly peaceful but ultimately deadly. The various rabbits represent many of humanity's traits of courage and resourcefulness, cruelty and evil. Art, music and mythology add to an entirely believable world which provokes discussion of wider issues such as the treatment of people and the abuses of society.
*Puffin* **P** 10 + years

# Time warps, space travel and future worlds

## A Rag, A Bone And A Hank Of Hair
*Nicholas Fisk*
In the twenty-first century, Brin lives in a society where youth are revered and the adults rarely have children. Brin is sent back to a simulated 1940 to monitor an experiment of chemically treated humans, the Reborns, who are capable of reproduction. Brin finds his life threatened after he develops sympathy with this earlier lifestyle.
*Puffin* **P** 10 + years

## The Makers
*Victor Kelleher*
Jeth is a warrior in a huge fortress set in a desert and ruled over by the aggressive, authoritarian Makers in a post-holocaust society. Jeth rebels and is cast out. Along with a young girl warrior, Jeth makes a dangerous trip to the Makers to demand freedom and justice. The reader is in for many surprises in this compelling science fiction novel which provokes much thought.
*Viking Kestrel* **H** 10 + years ☆

## White Mountains
*John Christopher*
One of the best and most satisfying works by this science fiction writer. Earth of the future is ruled by the Tripods, machine-like creatures from outer space, who implant a metal plate in humans to control their behaviour. Three boys reject the idea of the implant and run away, closely pursued by the Tripods. In the sequels, the boys fight the Tripods and conspire to save Earth from destruction.
Sequels in reading order: *The City Of Gold And Lead; The Pool Of Fire*
*Puffin* **P** 10–12 years

## A Wrinkle In Time
*Madeleine L'Engle*
Meg Murray's father, a government scientist, has disappeared to the planet, Camazotz, which is under the control of a pulsating brain. Meg, her brother Charles and a friend are variously tested for willpower and corruptibility. Exciting, dramatic and well-paced, this novel offers time-travel, alien planets and the danger of scientific experimentation.
Sequels in reading order: *A Wind In The Door; A Swiftly Tilting Planet*
*Puffin* **P** 10–12 years

## Conrad's War
*Andrew Davies*
Conrad objects to his father's career of writing romantic plays and dreams himself a grand hero in World War II. His fantasies come true! Conrad drives tanks against enemy soldiers and flies Lancasters but rebels at orders to machine-gun an ambulance. When Conrad becomes a prisoner of war, his infatuation with war begins to subside. The fantasy is totally believable and generates much excitement.
*Scholastic* **P** 10–12 years

## Halfway Across The Galaxy And Turn Left
*Robin Klein*
In this clever science fiction novel, X's family have been exiled from their planet after her father won the lottery a few too many times. Life is vastly different here, particularly because of role reversals and even parent/child reversals. X has previously been the Organiser of her family but eventually enjoys being as ordinary a twelve-year-old girl as possible. Some wildly funny scenes and lots of clever digs at earthlings.
*Puffin* **P** 10–14 years ☆

## Conrad
*Christine Nostlinger,*
A factory-made child, seven-year-old Conrad is perfect: he tells no lies and he is always polite, helpful and hard working. When he is delivered by mistake to Mrs Bartolotti, she eventually becomes accustomed to his ways and grows very fond of him. When the factory discovers its mistake and tries to reclaim Conrad, the only solution is to reprogram him into an ordinary child. These attempts add humour to a story which also has a serious message about conformity.
*Andersen* **P** 9–12 years

## Justice And Her Brothers
*Virginia Hamilton*
Justice, and her identical twin brothers, Thomas and Levi, are marked by those forces which strengthen inside them: telepathy, telekinesis and clairvoyance. The twins are able to interchange thoughts and physical selves but Thomas seeks more — to control both his brother and sister. The three decide to travel into the future together to find their role in life. In the sequels to follow, a chilling future is found and the children discover their lives in the present are essential to future survival.
Also: *Dustland; The Gathering*
*Julia MacRae* **H** 12 + years

### Aliens In The Family
*Margaret Mahy*
Jake feels like an outsider — an alien — when she visits her father's new family in New Zealand, but she soon discovers the realities of being a real alien when she meets Bond from another planet. As usual, Margaret Mahy's language bristles with exciting and original images and her plots have the reader glued to the page from beginning to end.
*Ashton Scholastic* **H**
10 + years

### Taronga
*Victor Kelleher*
After a nuclear war, Taronga Park Zoo in Sydney becomes an armed fortress, home to a violent, cruel group, protected by wild cats. Ben's ability to communicate with animals gains him entrance but he is tormented by the society's code of ethics. An open ending provokes thought.
*Viking Kestrel* **H**
11–13 years ☆

### Tangara
*Nan Chauncy, illustrated by Brian Wildsmith*
Lexie Pavemont resembles her great-great-Aunt Rita who befriended a young Tasmanian Aboriginal girl, Merrina. In a believable time-slip, Lexie and Merrina meet and play. The tragic destruction of Merrina's people by white Australians is re-enacted and witnessed by Lexie. The novel carries a powerful message about the mistreatment of Aborigines. It is also a memorable story of friendship and adventure.
*Puffin* **P** 9–12 years ☆

### Charlotte Sometimes
*Penelope Farmer*
Charlotte awakens one night at her new boarding school and discovers she has become Clare, a young girl who lived at the school some forty years earlier during World War I. Gripping and suspenseful, this is a fascinating read-aloud story.
*Puffin* **P** 10–12 years

### Playing Beatie Bow
*Ruth Park*
Victorian Sydney of 1873 and contemporary Sydney are successfully linked in this time-slip fantasy. Fourteen-year-old Abigail Kirk bitterly resents her parents' reunion after a marriage break-down and equally rejects living with her 'glittery and poisonous' grandmother. At this moment of stalemate, Abigail is transported back to 1873 and there learns the meaning of love and family affection. Fascinating details of life in this era are experienced through Abigail and the world created is as touchable as today's world. Immensely popular as a novel, the film adaptation ensures its popularity.
*Puffin* **P** 11–14 years ☆

### Tom's Midnight Garden
*Philippa Pearce*
Tom, quarantined with the measles, is sent to stay with his aunt and uncle. He is very bored until a grandfather clock strikes thirteen and a beautiful garden appears. There he meets young Hatty and, though a ghost himself in the past Victorian age, he becomes her companion. In a strange twist of plot, Hattie emerges as the adult owner of the flats where Tom is staying. The garden is her dream of the past and Tom's longing for companionship allows their lives to meet. An entirely believable time fantasy so well-detailed that the garden, Hattie and Tom exist for the reader.
*Puffin* **P** 10–12 years

# Realistic fiction

These are stories of daily life about children at home and school, coping with pesky siblings, troublesome bullies, important friends and influential parents and teachers. Themes of survival, friendship, loyalty, achievement and simply 'coming of age' all appear here. It's sometimes reassuring to know others have survived the traumas of childhood.

## Growing up

### All We Know
*Simon French*
Arkie, in her last year of primary school, is growing up and experiencing various human relationships. Explored are those of her mother with a new partner; friend Ian with a neglectful mother; and friend Kylie with new peers.
*Puffin* **P** 10–12 years ☆

### Handles
*Jan Mark*
Erica Timperley's great passion is motorbikes. During a holiday in the country, she discovers a motorbike repair shop and relishes a summer of adventure and self-discovery.
*Puffin* **P** 10–12 years

### Are You There God? It's Me, Margaret
*Judy Blume*
Eleven-year-old Margaret frequently addresses God on her problems: choosing a religion (her father is Jewish, her mother Catholic), adjusting to a move from New York to New Jersey and, most distressing, languishing over her slow physical maturation. Young girls find Margaret's concerns similar to their own and her frank, open expressions a mirror of their own private thoughts.
*Pan* **P** 10–12 years

### Eleanor, Elizabeth
*Libby Gleeson*
Eleanor resents a family move and finds it difficult to adjust to a new home, school and friends. Finding and reading her grandmother's diary gives Eleanor an insight into an earlier generation's similar difficulties and enables her to accept change.
*Puffin* **P** 10–12 years ☆

### Dear Emily
*Maureen Stewart*
Maria is a city-dweller who writes to Emily, her penpal in the country. Her lifestyle seems enviable, her possessions immense and her life full of happiness, particularly compared to a seemingly ho-hum existence in the country. The reader discovers that all is not what it appears in Maria's letters and gains an understanding of a confused young girl.
*Puffin* **P** 10–12 years ☆

### Granny Was A Buffer Girl
*Berlie Doherty*
Departing for a year of study in France, Jess feels scared yet thrilled. Three generations of the family come together to share their memories before she leaves. Tales of elopement, early deaths and life as a buffer girl in a cutlery firm are all shared with Jess, giving her strength and sustaining security.
*Collins Lion* **P** 10 + years

### I Am Susannah
*Libby Gleeson*
Susannah is nervous about going to high school and desperately misses an old friend. The author's literary craft and astute understanding of youth are evident as Susannah develops naturally.
*Angus & Robertson* **H** 10–12 years ☆

### The Min-Min
*Mavis Thorpe Clark*
Sylvia Edwards lives with her drunken father, physically ill mother, and brothers and sisters at a railway-workers' camp in the Australian outback. When her delinquent brother Reg wreaks havoc in the schoolroom, they run away together, hoping for help in building a new life. The plight of these young children and their runaway adventure in a harsh setting demand attention.
*Hodder & Stoughton* **P** 10–12 years ☆

### Summer Of The Swans
*Betsy Byars*
Fourteen-year-old Sara Godfrey is vaguely discontented with life and herself, a common complaint at this age. But her self-absorption is pushed aside when her younger brother, who is mentally disabled, goes missing as he tries to find swans on a lake he has seen earlier.
*Puffin* **P** 10–12 years

### The Road Ahead
*Lois Lowry*
Rabble was born under difficult circumstances. Her mother, sweet Hosanna, was only fourteen years old when Rabble was born. Her father left. Rabble and her mother live quite happily together over the Bigelow family's garage. Mother works as a housekeeper and babysitter for the Bigelows while Rabble and the Bigelow daughter are firm friends. When Mrs Bigelow becomes mentally ill, life changes but all the characters mature in a very satisfying story of relationships between family and friends.
*Houghton Mifflin* 🄷 10–12 years

*Incognito Mosquito, Private Insective*

## Adventure and survival

### Ash Road
*Ivan Southall*
Three city boys out camping foolishly light a fire which becomes a raging bushfire threatening an entire community. Various characters' reactions towards fear, danger and devastation are explored in this chilling, close-to-truth story.
*Puffin* 🄿 10–12 years ☆

### Incognito Mosquito, Private Insective
*E A Hass, illustrated by Don Madden*
Those who cannot resist word puns will thoroughly enjoy the exploits of the world's greatest 'insective'. This super sleuth's pursuits are satisfying, but the word puns are irresistibly funny.
*Random House* 🄿 9–11 years

### Deezle Boy
*Eleanor Spence*
Grant's passion for trains will strike a chord with others similarly inclined. Little does he expect to travel all over the Australian countryside away from his secure, protected environment, to a world of hotels and communes full of unusual people. Grant gradually, and believably, becomes more independent and learns much about security and family.
*Collins Dove* 🄿 10–12 years ☆

### The Fire In The Stone
*Colin Thiele*
Young Ernie Ryan ekes out a meagre living in an opal mining community in the desolate Australian desert. Ernie's opal find is stolen and his cash proceeds spent by his shiftless, alcoholic father. Further bad luck follows when Willie, Ernie's friend, dies from injuries he receives in a booby-trapped mine.
*Puffin* 🄿 11 + years ☆

### The Eighteenth Emergency
*Betsy Byars*
Mouse teases the school bully, Marv Hammerman, and now lives in mortal terror of the inevitable revenge. He and his friend Ezzie have devised incredible solutions to a range of emergencies but none are suitable. Finally mustering his courage and overcoming his fear, he faces Marv with surprising results.
*Puffin* 🄿 9–11 years

### From The Mixed-Up Files Of Mrs. Basil E. Frankweiler
*E L Konigsburg*
Claudia feels unappreciated and decides to run away from home with her younger brother Jamie. The ingenious aspect of this story is Claudia's desire to set up her new life in style — at New York's Metropolitan Museum of Art. Sleeping, eating and bathing present amusing challenges.
*Dell* 🄿 9–12 years

### Where The Lilies Bloom
*Vera and Bill Cleaver*
Fourteen-year-old Mary Call becomes head of the household when her father dies. She has great responsibility in caring for her young brother and retarded sister. Set in the Appalachian mountains, this novel has a beautiful setting, strong characters and an appealing theme of children surviving on their own resources.
*New American Library* 🅿
10–12 years

### The Incredible Journey
*Sheila Burnford,*
Animal lovers will thoroughly enjoy this classic tale of three pets, a Labrador retriever, a bull terrier and a Siamese cat, which travel 250 miles through the Canadian wilderness to be reunited with their owners. Perils along the way and how the animals cope make a gripping story.
*Hodder & Stoughton* 🅿
10 + years

### How To Eat Fried Worms
*Thomas Rockwell*
The revolting subject of this novel ensures great reader appeal and the humorous story delivers to the last page. Billy takes a bet to win a prize. The bet is that he cannot eat fifteen worms in fifteen days! Fortunately, dressings such as peanut butter and horseradish are allowed. Eventually Billy discovers a liking for worms!
*Pan* 🅿 9–11 years

### Julie Of The Wolves
*Jean Craighead George, Illustrated by Julek Heller*
This unforgettable survival story tells of a thirteen-year-old Eskimo girl's battle to live in the vast Alaskan tundra. With great patience and understanding she befriends a pack of wild wolves and joins their society. Not only is much revealed of Eskimo culture but of the wolves' lifestyle and the environment as well. Intensely riveting and enjoyable.
*Puffin* 🅿 10 + years

### People Might Hear You
*Robin Klein*
In this chilling story, inspired by actual similar events, a woman and her niece are lured by a mysterious religious sect to give up all contact with the outside world. Young Frances eventually rebels against the authoritarian rule but finds attempts to escape, if captured, mean total isolation and intensive social programming. Tense, suspenseful and compelling.
*Puffin* 🅿 10–14 years ☆

### Slake's Limbo
*Felice Holman*
Aremis Slake, aged thirteen, runs away from his abusive home life and threats from his peer group. For an amazing 121 days he survives in a New York subway tunnel. The writing style and characterisation create an utterly believable and memorable survival story.
*Collins Lion* 🅿 10–12 years

### Thursday's Child
*Noel Streatfeild, illustrated by Peggy Fortnum*
Orphan stories hold a special fascination. This one, set in late nineteenth century England, features Margaret Thursday, a particularly strong and resourceful orphan. She is the only orphan to run away from St Thomas's (taking two others with her), and the first girl to become a 'legger' on the canals. She even aspires to be an actress. Margaret is likeable and appealing and the background setting reveals English life at the turn of the century.
*Collins Lion* 🅿 9–12 years

### Homecoming
*Cynthia Voigt*
Thirteen-year-old Dicey is determined to find a home for herself and her younger siblings after their mother, suffering from mental illness, abandons them. They travel on foot to find a rich aunt who unfortunately has died, so they set off again to find a grandmother in Maryland whom they have never met. A secure and loving home is found but not without squabbles and difficulties. A long, involved story but one which exudes strength, warmth and fascinating characters.
Also: *Dicey's Song; Solitary Blue; Sons From Afar*
*Collins Lion* 🅿 10 + years

# Family and friends, home and school

### Cannily, Cannily
*Simon French*
Simon and his parents have spent seven of his eleven years travelling, so he has constantly changed schools and jobs. Battling yet again to be accepted by the group, Simon determines to succeed at football despite ignorance of the game. Persecution and harassment bedevil Simon until his parents realise his predicament.
*Puffin* 🅿 10 + years ☆

### Anne Of Green Gables
*Lucy M Montgomery*
This much-loved classic tells of Anne, a high-spirited, creative and mischievous orphan who is delivered to an elderly couple living on a farm on Prince Edward Island, Canada, in the late nineteenth century. They expect a boy, and so begins a series of mishaps which leave the reader taking Anne's side as she battles through school, teasing and an attachment to young Gilbert Blythe. Other titles in the series follow Anne's growth to womanhood.
*Angus & Robertson* 🅿
10–14 years

## Turbulent Term Of Tyke Tiler
*Gene Kemp*
Hilarious school stories have great appeal, especially with characters such as Tyke, bright and mischievous, and his friend Danny, who is mentally disabled. Tyke tries to coach Danny so he will not be sent to a special school, but ends up soaring so high himself that he may be sent to a school for the gifted. In a humorous finale, Tyke turns out to be female!
*Puffin* **P** 10–12 years

## Hating Alison Ashley
*Robin Klein*
Erica Yurken's air of superiority is shaken by the arrival of beautiful, intelligent and well-behaved Alison Ashley. School camp seems the perfect place to embarrass Alison until Erica discovers her envy is misplaced. Erica's hilarious views of life, overlay a poignant theme.
*Puffin* **P** 10 + years ☆

## Ordinary Jack
*Helen Cresswell*
In the madcap Bagthorpe family, everyone is multi-talented (although tempered by numerous foibles) except for poor Jack. Uncle Park tries to turn Jack into a prophet with hilarious results. There is plenty of fast-paced action in this witty story with numerous sequels.
*Puffin* **P** 10–12 years

## Superfudge
*Judy Blume*
Peter Hatcher, the hero of the popular novel, *Tales Of A Fourth Grade Nothing,* is now in the sixth grade and troubled as ever by his younger brother, four-year-old Fudgie. Peter's parents reveal a new baby is coming and a disruptive house move as well. Life is never simple or easy for Peter and the Hatcher family but the reader wholeheartedly enjoys their hilarious escapades.
*Pan* **P** 9–12 years

## Anastasia Krupnik
*Lois Lowry,*
Humorous, likeable real-life characters are in demand and ten-year-old Anastasia, who grows up in this series, fits the bill. She faces common experiences of children: a new sibling, a senile grandmother and life at home and school. The Krupnik family is sympathetic, supportive and well characterised and Anastasia's brother Sam is also an appealing addition.
*Collins Lion* **P** 9–11 years

## Harriet The Spy
*Louise Fitzhugh*
Harriet, an aspiring writer in sixth grade, spies on her friends and neighbours and jots down caustic notes in her journal. When her classmates discover Harriet's journal, they make her life miserable. Funny, sad and very inventive, this novel appeals especially for its fresh and lively heroine.
*Collins Lion* **P** 10–12 years

## Seven Little Australians
*Ethel Turner, illustrated by Sandra Laroche*
First published in 1894, this family story, continues to have appeal today. Family life, with all its ups and downs, is very believable and a number of the children draw great sympathy from the reader. Most memorable is a death scene where one of the children dies. No reader emerges untouched.
*Angus & Robertson* **H**
10 + years ☆

## The Green Wind
*Thurley Fowler*
An Australian farm setting of the 1940s offers a fascinating, humorous portrait of a family with appealing, universal characters. Jennifer, who is eleven, insecure and prickly, envies her sister Margaret. Alexander is overly sensitive and Richard is ashamed of his father, whose prisoner-of-war experiences affect the entire family.
*Rigby* **P** 10–12 years ☆

### Five Times Dizzy
*Nadia Wheatley, illustrated by Neil Phillips*
Mareka's grandmother has recently arrived from Greece to join her son and his family. Their delicatessen in Newtown and its surrounding neighbourhood is so alien that grandmother appears to age daily. Mareka thinks of a brilliant plan to enrich her grandmother's life. Community life is well portrayed with its aspects of prejudice and tolerance revealed.
*Oxford University Press*
9–12 years ☆

### Nothing's Fair In Fifth Grade
*Barthe DeClements*
Friendless Elsie is scorned by her mother and turns to food for comfort. When her mother puts her on a strict diet, she steals money for food from her fifth grade classmates. Caught and threatened with expulsion and boarding school, Elsie is thoroughly despondent until her friends and an understanding teacher come to her aid. Classroom and playground cruelty, friendship between children, and home life are totally real in this satisfying novel.
Also: *Sixth Grade Can Really Kill You*
*Scholastic* 9–12 years

### Bridge To Terabithia
*Katherine Paterson*
Jess relinquishes the honour of being the fastest runner in the fifth grade when Leslie, a newcomer, arrives in his rural Virginia community. They become inseparable, despite their different backgrounds, and create an imaginary kingdom, Terabithia. Leslie is accidentally drowned and the reader is deeply moved in this unforgettable story of friendship. Mood illustrations effectively capture the settings and deep anguish.
*Puffin* 10–12 years

*Five Times Dizzy*

### I Own The Racecourse
*Patricia Wrightson*
Andy is mentally disabled, but he is a firm part of a group of neighbourhood boys. They accept Andy for himself and generally he joins all their activities. But when Andy misunderstands their make-believe game of owning public property, he believes he has bought the Sydney racecourse for three dollars. Trouble erupts when Andy begins to 'improve' his property. The solution to this problem is clever. Readers will enjoy the superb characterisation and the solving of a tricky problem.
*Puffin* 10–12 years ☆

# Family problems

### The Cabby's Daughter
*David Martin*
Bess Tillick is a survivor; she has to be. A gambling, drunken father, no mother, a younger brother and a small country town in the Australian bush in 1903 all add to her problems. Bess tells her own captivating story, revealing not only hardships but humorous events as well.
*Hodder & Stoughton*
10–14 years ☆

### Dear Mr Henshaw
*Beverly Cleary*
Leigh Botts, aged ten, writes to his favourite author then later records in a journal his emotional turmoil over his parents' divorce and a new school. There is light humour throughout and a strong empathy develops between the reader and young Leigh .
*Puffin* 10–12 years

### So Much To Tell You...
*John Marsden*
Through diary entries, Marina slowly reveals the cause of her mute condition: her father disfigured her face with acid meant for her mother. Marina is placed in a girls' boarding school and there begins her recovery through an understanding teacher, counsellor and peers.
*Walter McVitty Books*
11–13 years ☆

## A Tide Flowing
*Joan Phipson*
Ten-year-old Mark Taylor and his mother sail for England to visit her family, but the mother's devastating death at sea changes the boy's life. Mark goes to live with his paternal grandparents in Sydney and suffers again when his father rejects him for a new life. Not until Mark is fifteen and meets Connie, a quadriplegic, is he able to share his deepest thoughts and prepare for the future.
*Ashton Scholastic* **P**
10 + years ☆

## Don't Hurt Laurie!
*Willo Davis Roberts*
Since she was three, Laurie has been abused by her mother and only her stepbrother knows. When her mother attacks a puppy, Laurie runs away and gets help both for herself and her mother. The emotions, fears and traumas are sensitively handled.
*Macmillan* **P** 10 + years

## The Great Gilly Hopkins
*Katherine Paterson*
Eleven-year-old Gilly has developed a crusty exterior and a manipulative, hostile personality due to a history of abandonment and a series of unsuccessful foster homes. It is Maine Trotter's capacity for love, in yet another foster home, that breaks through to Gilly. A satisfying story full of well-developed characters, crisp dialogue and lively humour.
*Puffin* **P** 10–12 years

## The Left Overs
*Eleanor Spence*
Four children aged eight to eleven are wards of the state. When news arrives that their home is to be demolished and they are to be separated, the two oldest children concoct elaborate schemes to draw attention to their plight. Humour, adventure and strong characters have strong appeal.
*Ashton Scholastic* **P** 9–12 years ☆

## The Not-Just-Anybody Family
*Betsy Byars*
Maggie and Vern Blossom are faced with unravelling family troubles — Grandpa is gaoled for disturbing the peace and Junior has two broken legs. Family misfortunes are overcome by love and loyalty. This rather unusual family continues its wacky existence with oddball characters in other novels.
*Pan* **P** 10–12 years

## The October Child
*Eleanor Spence, illustrated by Malcolm Green*
The trials of caring for an autistic child within the family are realistically explored in this story. Parental frustration and conflict appear, but young Douglas is the primary focus as he, more than his siblings, relates to Carl. Emotions of jealousy, guilt and rage are believably portrayed
*Oxford University Press* **P** 9–12 years ☆

## One-Eyed Cat
*Paula Fox*
Ned receives an air rifle from his uncle as a birthday present, but his father forbids him to use it. Use it he does, sneaking out one night and taking a shot at a shadow. Later he is overwhelmed with guilt, suspecting that he has wounded a one-eyed feral cat. Tension mounts as Ned tries to care for the cat and continues to harbour his guilt.
*Puffin* **P** 10–12 years

## The Pinballs
*Betsy Byars*
Three neglected and abused children reluctantly come together in a foster home. Each one has a horrific tale to tell and suffers from deep-seated insecurities. While the plot sounds depressing, there are moments of hilarity, deeply satisfying emotions and a wholly comforting resolution.
*Puffin* **P** 10–12 years

# Picture books for older readers

Not all picture books are designed for young children. Authors and illustrators occasionally tackle complex concepts like war and peace, pollution, progress and eternity. A critical eye is beamed on scientists, politicians and society's 'protectors' — the military, police and firefighters. Illustrations are often sophisticated, requiring some knowledge of art or visual symbols. These picture books are thought-provoking, memorable and great discussion starters.

## Moon Man
*Tomi Ungerer*
Bored with life on the moon, Moon Man looks down with envy upon the dancing Earth people. But when a shooting star allows him to travel to Earth, his arrival is considered an invasion. The treatment of outsiders by a suspicious and cruel society is an underlying theme.
*Methuen* **P** 6–10 years

## The Big Green Book
*Robert Graves, illustrated by Maurice Sendak*
Every child wishes for a magic spell to learn lessons instantaneously. Jack learns such a spell from the big green book then plays tricks on his aunt and uncle, his dog and rabbit. But eventually he realises that magic can be dangerous.Wish fulfilment and witty line illustrations ensure this tale an audience.
*Puffin* **P** 5–10 years

## River
*Charles Keeping*
Several messages underlie this wordless view of the creation and demolition of human constructions. Against a single backdrop, various buildings are constructed. Graffiti on the buildings, the sculpture in front, the various human activities: all comment on human values and endeavours throughout history.
*Oxford University Press* **H** 9 + years

## The Butter Battlebook
*Dr Seuss*
Through his usual zany imaginative characters and catchy verse, Seuss poses a frightening question: Who will be the first to drop the bomb? The Yooks and Zooks live on opposite sides of a high stone wall, their differences highlighted by one group eating their bread with the butter on top and the other with the butter on the bottom. Such a minor difference causes great conflict .
*Collins* **P** All ages

## The Hiroshima Story
*Toshi Maruki*
Full-page impressionistic paintings of the human devastation caused by the bomb dropped on Hiroshima are not for the fainthearted. The tale is told from seven-year-old Mii's point of view which renders this anti-war message more potent.
*Black* **H** 10 + years

## Dinosaurs And All That Rubbish
*Michael Foreman*
The message is direct: care for the Earth and its creatures for it belongs to all. A man dreams of travelling to a distant star and exerts all his efforts towards this goal, neglecting the Earth and destroying the ecology. The distant star proves barren and the man heads for another. Meanwhile, ancient dinosaurs have emerged and restored Earth's beauty. The man sees his error in neglecting Earth and vows to change. Paradise has been his all along!
*Puffin* **P** 5–10 years

## Come Away From The Water, Shirley
*John Burningham*
While Shirley's parents laze on the beach and warn their daughter of smelly seaweed, strange dogs and filthy tar, Shirley has an amazing imaginative adventure with pirates. This is a send-up of parents, but also a story of Shirley's imaginative world.
*Collins* **P** 5–9 years

## Magical Changes
*Graham Oakley*
Highly inventive images are created by pages which are split in half. Each turn of the page brings a new combination in view with amusing and often unexpected possibilities. No words accompany these illustrations, but none are needed.
*Macmillan* **H** 10–12 years

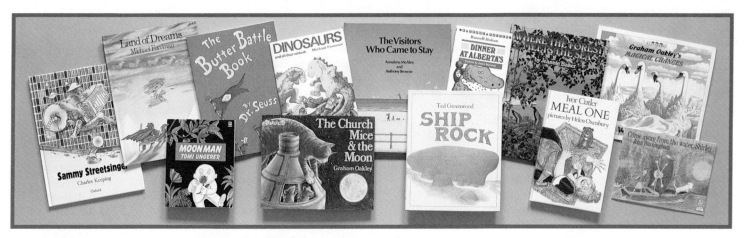

## The Church Mice And The Moon

*Graham Oakley*

Arthur and Humphrey, leaders of the church mice, are kidnapped by two scientists to be trained as astronauts. Sampson, the church cat, discovers their whereabouts and secures their rescue in an amusing way. The illustrations add innumerable humorous details which show various community attitudes to space exploration, and the stupidity of scientists and politicians.

*Macmillan* **P** 7–10 years

## Dinner At Alberta's

*Russell Hoban, illustrated by James Marshall*

Arthur Crocodile is unconcerned about his dreadful table manners until the lovely Alberta comes to visit. Arthur is bewitched. Droll illustrations of a love-sick alligator and family efforts to cultivate manners add great humour to this morality tale.

*Puffin* **P** 5–10 years

## Where The Forest Meets The Sea

*Jeannie Baker*

The shrinking rainforest in Australia's north Queensland inspired the artist to construct an imaginative story of a young boy exploring the wilderness beauty and pondering its possible demise. Striking relief collages effectively link past, present and future.

*Julia McRae* **H** 5 + years ☆

## Land Of Dreams

*Michael Foreman*

What happens to all the unfinished, forgotten dreams and hopes of humans? In this story, they are reassembled by an old man and a boy who live high in the mountains. Thereafter the dreams are released to drift around the world making people smile. A magical idea which is enhanced by glowing watercolours.

*Hodder & Stoughton* **P** 7 + years

## Meal One

*Ivor Cutler, illustrated by Helen Oxenbury*

Herbert's mother is different, she plays football, fights and digs holes with her son. There's an unusual surprise ending to top off this humorous portrayal of family life.

*Collins Lion* **P** 5–9 years

## The Visitors Who Came To Stay

*Annalena McAfee, illustrated by Anthony Browne*

Mary is accustomed to a quiet, regulated life with Dad all to herself, so when vivacious Kate and her trick-playing son come to stay, there is inevitable confusion. Eventually Mary blurts out she liked life better the old way and the two visitors leave. Life somehow seems empty now and Mary changes her mind. The illustrations show objects out of place and joined in impossible combinations.

*Hamish Hamilton* **P** 7–12 years

## Ship Rock

*Ted Greenwood*

A huge rock attracts tourists who climb over it, carve on it and conjure up ceremonies of times past. The role of the rock as host for plants, refuge for small animals and provider of nutrients for life is captured in soft, crayon-like textured illustrations. A thought-provoking exploration of eternity and ecology.

*Hutchinson* **H** 7 + years ☆

## Sammy Streetsinger

*Charles Keeping*

Sammy Streetsinger leads a simple, happy life as a subway performer until he is discovered by unscrupulous individuals who mould him to fit their own images of success. But success brings loneliness, failure and unhappiness for Sammy until he returns to his former life. Illustrations are psychedelic and sophisticated.

*Oxford University Press* **H** 10–13 years

### The Shrinking Of Treehorn

*Florence Parry Heide, illustrated by Edward Gorey*

Treehorn notices an alarming phenomenon — he's shrinking! 'But nobody shrinks', declares his father. Here is a biting satire on adults who are inept at solving problems, too busy to listen and too prone to ignore small children. Each page has witty, appealing line illustrations. Also: *Treehorn's Treasure*

*Puffin* **P** 5–9 years

### Trick A Tracker

*Michael Foreman*

Two themes are offered here: humanity's relentless pursuit of animals and the 'rat race' of progress. Animals are forced to pool ideas to ensure their survival against hunters. Obsessed with movement the humans leave their tracking pursuits behind and become truck drivers, speed cops, road hogs and the like.

*Macmillan* **P** 7 + years

### Stringbean's Trip To The Shining Sea

*Vera B Williams and Jennifer Williams*

Stringbean recounts his trip from Kansas to the Pacific coast using an original and innovative format. All is revealed through postcards and snapshots arranged in an album. A great book for encouraging children to chronicle their own lives.

*Greenwillow* **H** 9–12 years

### When The Wind Blows

*Raymond Briggs*

James and Hilda Bloggs are innocent victims of their own ignorance, misinformation and the follies of warring humans. When news of a bomb is broadcast, the Bloggs enter their homemade shelter, a woeful excuse for protection. Using a comic strip format, which belies the seriousness of the subject, Briggs forces the viewer to witness the couple's slow, inevitable death. Illustrations begin in varied colours and decline to a sickly, drab olive and tan. No doubt this book is meant to provoke action or, at the very least, to arouse strong debate.

*Puffin* **P** 9–13 years

### Panda's Puzzle

*Michael Foreman*

One day a panda discovers a deserted campsite and puzzles over a can with a picture of tall buildings and a black-and-white bear. He travels through China, Egypt, the United States, the Himalayas and the Far East to find out whether he is a black bear with white bits or a white bear with black bits. Everyone he meets has their own concept of what makes them what they are. Subtle comments on human nature and widely accepted homilies abound. Superb watercolours effectively reflect the various countries through which Panda travels.

*Puffin* **P** 8–10 years

### My Hiroshima

*Junko Morimoto*

Junko Morimoto personally experienced the bombing of Hiroshima and this is her story of that day, recollected as a child's memories. Early illustrations reveal happy times, then increasingly a military build-up in Japan. Absent from school the day of the bomb, Morimoto recalls crawling from the ruins of her house to view terrible destruction and human suffering. Impressionistic paintings evoke a sense of horror. A book for sharing and discussion.

*Collins* **H** 9 + years ☆

### The Mysteries Of Harris Burdick

*Chris Van Allsburg*

Fourteen full-page, black-and-white illustrations appear, each with a cryptic title and explanatory caption. Yet each contains a mystery: bizarre, eerie or incredible. Illustrations, titles, captions — sometimes at odds with each other — add to the awesome mood.

*Andersen* **H** All ages

### Anno's Journey

*Mitsumasa Anno*

Anno's series of journey books appeal to all ages. Each book follows a similar format: the reader follows an individual's journey through countryside, village and town with various stories occurring along the way.

*Bodley Head* **H** All ages (Library)

### La Corona And The Tin Frog

*Russell Hoban, illustrated by Nicola Bayley*

At the magical stroke of twelve o'clock, mysterious events occur: a tin frog disappears into a picture, a tin horseman breaks an enchantment and a wooden night-watchman writes poetry. The clock observes all these events and determines that time must be freed. Each of the three tales is philosophical with such ideas as life is only a treadmill, time only exists for the present and fear is courage. Illustrations have a haunting, mystical quality and highlight a lengthy text.

*Jonathan Cape* **H** 5–8 years (Library)

### The Sea People

*Jorg Steiner, illustrated by Jorg Muller*

Two adjacent islands vary greatly. One is inhabited by tall people, some masters and some slaves, who work long and hard to have beautiful lands and buildings. The other is occupied by small people, all of equal stature and all living happily. The King of the Greater Island almost destroys the Lesser Island, until a strange twist of plot reverses the fortunes of the two islands. A tale of greed, cruelty and inhumanity with evocative, naturalistic illustrations.

*Gollancz* **H** 9–11 years

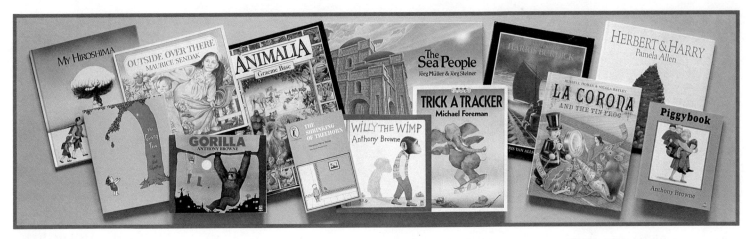

## Piggybook
*Anthony Browne*
Life is pretty gruelling for Mrs Piggott who does all the cooking, cleaning and washing — all juggled with an outside job. 'You are pigs,' Mrs Piggott declares in a letter to her family and leaves them to survive on their own. Browne's illustrations prove they are pigs indeed! Mrs Piggott returns but on her own terms in this satire on sex roles.
*Methuen* **P** 6 + years

## Outside Over There
*Maurice Sendak*
While Mama watches and waits for her husband away at sea, young Ida looks after the baby. But mysterious goblins kidnap the baby and Ida must rescue her. The paintings, which have multiple meanings, are arresting and invite the reader to puzzle over the interplay of the real and the imagined.
*Puffin* **P** 7 + years

## The Giving Tree
*Shel Silverstein*
A tree develops a relationship with a young boy, giving him apples to eat, limbs to climb, leaves to gather and shade for napping. As the boy matures and his needs change, he takes other things from the tree: apples to sell for money; branches to build a house and finally the trunk itself to build a boat. The nature of love, friendship and sacrifice are poignantly explored.
*Jonathan Cape* **H** 6 + years

## Gorilla
*Anthony Browne*
A lonely young girl is comforted by gorilla paraphernalia. One night a gorilla appears at the foot of her bed and takes her on a marvellous adventure. The surreal illustrations are very sophisticated, requiring knowledge beyond that of a child, yet the story speaks simply, too, of loneliness.
*Magnet* **P** 8 + years

## Herbert And Harry
*Pamela Allen*
Two brothers live and work happily together until they discover a treasure. In a scuffle, Herbert wins the treasure and takes it far away to the top of a mountain, defended by a fortress with many guns. His years are spent guarding the treasure while his brother Harry lives happily surrounded by his family.
The theme of greed and the effects of hoarding are clearly outlined in this parable.
*Nelson* **H** 6–9 years ☆

## War And Peas
*Michael Foreman*
King Lion's people are starving for the land is dry and nothing will grow. Nearby are neighbours with an oversupply of food but unwilling to share it. In an amusing twist to this satire on greed, the land again becomes fertile and greed is punished.
*Puffin* **P** 7 + years

## Willy The Wimp
*Anthony Browne*
Willy the gorilla sends off for a book which promises to transform him — bulging muscles, magnetic personality and so on. Through diet and exercise, Willie becomes a 'new man'. Then he awkwardly bumps into a lamp post and utters an apology. The message is clear: changing outer appearances does not alter the person inside.
Also: *Willy The Champ*
*Magnet* **P** 5–8 years

## Animalia
*Graeme Base*
A sumptuous book for all ages. Each letter of the alphabet is illustrated with various objects beginning with the same letter — some easy to spot, others camouflaged. For the very youngest viewer, there is a small boy hidden in each illustration. Here's a game book of great visual appeal.
*Viking Kestrel* **H** All ages ☆

**83**

# Historical fiction

In these books readers may experience life through a young character's perspective in such fascinating periods as those of the Salem witch trials, seventeenth century plagues, World War II, Viking and pioneer times. The historical detail is so intricately embedded in these fascinating stories that the reader is able to 'live' through these times.

## Blood Feud
*Rosemary Sutcliff*
A master storyteller of historical fiction relates, from English Jestyn's point of view, the tenth century Viking way of life.
*Puffin* **P** 10 + years

## A Gathering Of Days: A New England Girl's Journal, 1830–1832
*Joan W Blos*
Through entries in her journal, Catherine's fourteenth year naturally unfolds. Life on a New Hampshire farm is interestingly detailed, while relationships with a new stepmother and old friends, plus her own developing self-awareness, make this a believable story of life in earlier times.
*Atheneum* **P** 10 + years

## The Apprentices
*Leon Garfield*
Garfield knows how to select details that bring eighteenth century England to life. These apprentices are lively, well-rounded characters and each has a moment of trial set against the sights, smells and customs of the day. Line illustrations which provide authentic, historical detail.
*Puffin* **P** 10 + years

## Dragonwings
*Lawrence Yep*
Drawing on his own experiences as a third generation Chinese American, Yep bases this story of an early twentieth century aeroplane flight on a true incident. Moon Shadow Lee leaves China to join his father, who is building a plane, in San Francisco's Chinatown in 1903. Life in this era with its Chinese society, brotherhoods, opium dens, an earthquake and clash of cultures is fascinating.
*Harper & Row* **P** 10 + years

## A Parcel Of Patterns
*Jill Walsh*
Using actual historical records, Walsh recreates the tragic outbreak of the plague in the seventeenth century Derbyshire village of Eyam. The story is told through the memoirs of young Mall Percival who documents the town's voluntary isolation.
*Puffin* **P** 10 + years

## Roll Of Thunder, Hear My Cry
*Mildred Taylor*
The setting is Mississippi during the Depression. The family is the Logans, blacks who are economically deprived and cruelly mistreated. The story is narrated by young Cassie who recounts her family's battle to retain self-respect and independence. An unforgettable tale, richly embroidered with characters, dialogue and settings that linger in the mind.
*Puffin* **P** 10 + years

## Island Of The Blue Dolphins
*Scott O'Dell*
This classic story of a young girl's survival against extreme loneliness and constant perils is based on a true story of a young woman abandoned by her tribe on a remote Californian island for eighteen years. One of the most enduring of all survival stories written for children.
*Puffin* **P** 9–12 years

## Little House In The Big Woods
*Laura Ingalls Wilder, illustrated by Garth Williams*
No child should miss this warm family series covering nine novels about an American pioneer family. In this first novel, Laura and her family live in their small house in Wisconsin in 1870 after leaving their home in New York State. Aspects of daily life are so vivid and detailed, based as they are on the author's own childhood, that the reader lives each day with this family.
*Puffin* **P** 9–12 years

## The Silver Sword
*Ian Serraillier, illustrated by C Walter Hodges*
Three Polish children are separated from their parents following the Nazi invasion of their country in 1940. They are forced to fend for themselves until liberation of their city in 1945. A long-time favourite and a classic adventure story.
*Puffin* **P** 10 + years

## Acacia Terrace
*Barbara Ker Wilson, illustrated by David Fielding*
Australian history is traced through the lives of successive families living in a row of terrace houses in Sydney. Fielding's naive illustrations range from goldrush camps to modern cityscapes and are detailed and witty.
*Ashton Scholastic* **H**
12 + years ☆

## The Angel With The Mouth-Organ
*Christobel Mattingley, illustrated by Astra Lacis*
The struggles of a refugee family in Europe during World War II are told through the limited perspective of a young child. While fear and hate are present, the positive emotions of courage and love emerge as more powerful through strong family unity. Illustrations very effectively portray the devastation.
*Hodder & Stoughton* **P**
7–10 years ☆

## The Chinese Boy
*David Martin*
Few children's novels portray the Australian gold fields of the 1860s so vividly. From his Chinese perspective, fourteen-year-old Ho views the harsh, often violent life style in Kiandra in the Australian Alps. Appealing and colourful episodes and characters abound. Alternating examples of warm humanity and cold brutality strengthen the underlying theme of racial prejudice.
*Hodder & Stoughton* **P**
10–14 years ☆

## The Lark And The Laurel
*Barbara Willard*
Set in Great Britain during the reign of Richard III, this novel traces the fortunes of young Cecily Jolland, brought up at Mantlemass Manor.
A memorable novel with sequels which are strong on character and setting.
*Kestrel* **H** 11 + years

## Longtime Passing
*Hesba Brinsmead*
Although fiction, this novel is closely based on the author's family reminiscences of life in the Blue Mountains, west of Sydney. Using an episodic, anecdotal style, Brinsmead reveals pioneering life of the 1930s in a warm, extended family.
*Angus & Robertson* **P**
9–11 years ☆

## The Machine Gunners
*Robert Westall*
Set during World War II, this novel involves a small town in northern England which is daily bombed by German planes. When young Chas discovers a machine-gun in a downed plane, suspense builds. Chas drags the gun to an underground shelter. A German soldier stumbles upon the shelter and offers information on the gun in exchange for help in escaping. Taut, compelling reading.
*Puffin* **P** 10 + years

## Ox-Cart Man
*Donald Hall, illustrated by Barbara Cooney*
Family life in nineteenth century rural New England is simply and effectively told through illustrations and a simple text. All that the family produces beyond their own needs, the ox-cart man takes by wagon to Portsmouth market. The illustrations are filled with informative details of life in this era
*Puffin* **P** 7–9 years

## The Sign Of The Beaver
*Elizabeth George Speare*
Matt, almost thirteen, is left alone in the family's new cabin in Maine while his father brings the rest of the family into this pioneer setting of 1768. Trouble comes in large doses when Matt's gun is stolen, a bear takes his food supplies and he is attacked by bees. He is saved by Indians and so begins a friendship and a respect for cultural traditions.
*Gollancz* **H** 10 + years

# Non-fiction

Non-fiction books today are visually exciting with lively, informative and accurate texts which stimulate thinking and encourage further investigation. Included here are fascinating books which beg to be read from cover to cover with their myriad topics of current interest and historical and cultural importance. Try one yourself! Sometimes the clearest introduction to a topic is a children's book!

## Leonardo da Vinci
*Alice and Martin Provensen*
Leonardo's major accomplishments as artist, engineer, and astronomer are very effectively captured in this pop-up book. Useful for stimulating interest in this genius.
*Viking* 🄷 9–11 years

## Everlasting Circle
*Ted Greenwood*
The shearwater chick's birth, growth, winter migration and summer regeneration of life is told in flowing blank verse and shown in highly textured drawings on cream paper.
*Hutchinson* 🄷 7–9 years ☆

## The Land I Lost
*Huynh Quang Nhuong, illustrated by Vor Dinh Mai*
This true story of the author's childhood in a Vietnamese village before the outbreak of war details numerous episodes in his life. His relationship with his cousin and pet water buffalo, adventures with various animals and his strong attachment for his land all reveal much about Vietnamese culture.
*Harper & Row* 🄷 10–13 years

## Mischling, Second Degree
*Ilse Koehn*
As an adult, Ilse Koehn learnt her parents separated to spare her the consequences of having a Jewish parent during the Nazi regime in World War II. Ilse was drafted into the Hitler Youth and learned to survive by pretending loyalty. This is a tale of the fears and hardships faced by the young in the Hitler Youth camps.
*Puffin* 🄿 10 + years

## Introducing Margaret Mahy
*Betty Gilderdale, illustrated by Alan Gilderdale*
Reading about one's favourite author is always a fascinating experience and as Margaret Mahy writes for all ages, there is something here to interest many. Most interesting are the revelations about Margaret Mahy that relate to the inspiration and incidents in her books. Her experiences as a children's librarian and writer are also told. Illustrations show objects in Mahy's house.
*Viking Kestrel* 🄷 9–12 years

## Albert Einstein
*Milton Dank*
Einstein's life and discoveries are skilfully interwoven. The author shows Einstein to be a humanitarian and a scientist devoted to his work. His discoveries are further detailed in an appendix.
*Franklin Watts* 🄷 10 + years

## Ant Cities
*Arthur Dorros*
A fascinating study of ants which inspires further investigation. Responsibilities of the queen, males and workers are explained together with their life cycle, care of eggs, various species and eating habits. Appealing crayon drawings, an enjoyable text, appropriate terminology and clear labelling are valuable features. Instructions for making an ant farm add appeal.
*Crowell* 🄷 5–8 years

## Why Are We Getting A Divorce?
*Peter Mayle, illustrated by Arthur Robins*
This team has produced a number of successful books on sexuality and parenthood. Divorce is treated here with sensitivity and understanding. Why parents divorce and how to maintain relationships with both parents are issues explored with commonsense advice.
*Harmony* 🄷 8–12 years ☆

## Boy: Tales Of Childhood
*Roald Dahl*
Roald Dahl relates his childhood in his usual captivating and exhilarating style. A strong feature is Dahl's English school experiences which reveal strong discipline set against a wilful youth. Each episode in Dahl's life makes a fascinating story in itself and this author's many fans will revel in the boyish pranks.
*Puffin* 🄿 10 + years

**Doctor Hunger And Captain Thirst: Stories Of Australian Explorers**
*Meredith Hooper*
Fifteen exploring expeditions of the nineteenth century are presented in fascinating detail through documents, diaries, paintings and drawings of the time. A combined documentary and narrative style brings these explorers' efforts to life.
*Methuen* H 10–12 years (Library) ☆

**Francis, The Poor Man Of Assisi**
*Tomie de Paola*
Francis Di Bernardone, son of a rich merchant, denounced his lifestyle and embraced the worship of God and extreme poverty. Miracles which inspired him, those which he performed and the founding of the order Little Sisters of the Poor are all recounted. Muted colours reflect the gentle nature of Francis of Assisi.
*Holiday House* H 9–11 years

**Sadako And The Thousand Paper Cranes**
*Eleanor Coerr*
Ten years after the atomic bomb was dropped on Hiroshima, young Sadako Sasaki died from leukaemia, a fatal disease caused by radiation poisoning. Sadako's story is one of great courage and hope, symbolised by her belief in a legendary story of a golden crane.
*Hodder & Stoughton* P 9–11 years

**You Won't Believe Your Eyes!**
*Pat Robbins (ed)*
Visual illusions both natural and human-made are covered in five exciting chapters on the interaction of brain and eye to create vision: illusions created by artists; cinematic effects and illusions by architects and advertisers; nature's illusions; and magic involving illusions. Full colour photographs and drawings are accompanied by a fascinating text.
*National Geographic Society* H 8–12 years

**Helen Keller**
*Margaret Davidson, illustrated by Wendy Watson*
Helen Keller's lack of sight and hearing were so frustrating for her that her childhood was extremely difficult for herself and those around her until a teacher, Annie Sullivan, broke through these barriers. Helen Keller obtained an education and became an outstanding political figure, lobbying for the disabled, women and civil rights.
*Scholastic* P 7–10 years

**Up Goes The Skyscraper!**
*Gail Gibbons*
Gibbons specialises in making complex processes understandable to very young children. This book explains why and how skyscrapers are built, along with the workers and their individual tasks. The prose is simple and the illustrations clear and appealing.
*Macmillan* H 5–8 years

**The Diary Of Anne Frank**
*Anne Frank*
Thirteen-year-old Anne records the daily existence of two Jewish families forced into hiding during World War II. It is a moving portrait of an adolescent striving to understand her family and her emerging feelings for a young boy. Its setting against desperate and real wartime conditions adds a special strength to this timeless story of youth growing up.
*Pan* P 10 + years

**Fox On My Door**
*David Martin, illustrated by Jay Martin*
David Martin has made a significant contribution to Australian children's literature with his sensitive and serious but often rollicking adventures of those who are different in society. Here he takes the reader through his life as a twin growing up in Germany, experiences in the Spanish Civil War, Greece, India and other places.
*Collins Dove* P 10–12 years ☆

**Building For Kids And Adventurous Adults**
*John Archer*
Detailed line drawings and photographs will inspire budding builders. Simple structures and inexpensive materials are emphasised. A glossary and further sources of information are included.
*Oxford University Press* P 9–12 years (Library) ☆

**The Story Of Australia**
*Don Watson*
Australia's history from prehistoric times to the present is told in a highly readable style. Famous people and events feature but so, too, do ordinary Australians. Aboriginal history is a major topic treated. Time lines preceding each chapter relate Australian and world events.
*Nelson* H 10–12 years (Library) ☆

**To Space And Back**
*Sally Ride and Susan Okie*
Sally Ride provides a personal account of her trip in space including not only the spectacular aspects but such mundane details as how lunch is prepared and what can be seen from the window. The exterior colour photographs are exceptional and include some cosy snapshots of the spacecraft interior.
*Lothrop* H 6–12 years

**The Human Body: How We Evolved**
*Joanna Cole, illustrated by Walter Gaffney-Kessell and Juan Carlos Barberis*
In a fascinating style, Cole covers a comparison of the human body with modern and ancient primates; a detailed examination of such aspects as the pelvis, toe, eye and teeth, their evolution and function. Clear, informative diagrams and sketches, along with charts and time lines, are features of this excellent book.
*Morrow* H 7–11 years (Library)

## From Hand To Mouth: Or, How We Invented Knives, Forks, Spoons, And Chopsticks And The Table Manners To Go With Them

*James Cross Giblin*

This fascinating history shows that eating utensils developed from common sense and propriety. The use of each eating utensil is shown in photographs, reproductions and line drawings.

*Crowell* **H** 9–12 years (Library)

## A Look At Computers

*Jack Winch and John McCarney*

A good, general introduction to the applications and implications of computers in today's society. A variety of activities featured at the end of each section

*Addison-Wesley* **P** 10 + years

## The Ashton Scholastic History Of Australia

*Manning Clark and Meredith Hooper, illustrated by Susanne Ferrier*

Historian Manning Clark's notable six-volume work for adults has been rewritten, with other sources added, for children, resulting in a narrative history both interesting and accessible in style. Accompanying illustrations are attractive and informative. The condensation of material and limited coverage after 1950 necessitates the use of additional resources.

*Ashton Scholastic* **P**
8–12 years ☆

## Journey To The Planets

*Patricia Lauber*

Lauber's science books are particularly outstanding and this one is no exception. After an introduction to the Earth, Lauber covers each satellite and planet in our solar system. Information gleaned from American and Soviet space explorations, Earth experiments and new theories are covered. Magnificent black-and-white photographs and line drawings are valuable.

*Crown* **H** 10 + years (Library)

## The Arrow Book Of Backyard Creatures

*Brian Mackness*

This entertaining book is full of information and activities relevant to the creatures found in every backyard. Beautiful colour photographs highlight the text.
Also: *The Arrow Book Of Bush Creatures*
*Ashton Scholastic* **P**
8–10 years ☆

## Pompeii: Exploring A Roman Ghost Town

*Ron and Nancy Goor*

The eruption of Mt Vesuvius in 79 AD and the subsequent burial of the Roman town, Pompeii, is one of the most fascinating true stories of all time. Here presented brilliantly is the story beginning with the only eyewitness account, an analysis of this natural disaster and a final tour of the resurrected ruins.

*Crowell* **H** 9 + years

## How Does Your Garden Grow?

*Kevin Heinze, illustrated by Bob Graham*

An inspirational guide for young gardeners beginning with the essential tools and basic information on soil, plants and pests. Style is highly readable and illustrations are informative and lighthearted.

*Five Mile Press* **P**
8–12 years ☆

## My Place

*Nadia Wheatley, illustrated by Donna Rawlins*

This highly original book traces Australian history from 1988 back to 1788. Each double-page spread steps back ten years, always at the same site, and reveals life at that time through the perspective of a child living there. Social and historical events are revealed in the excellent illustrations and briefly alluded to in the text. The entire book is a superlative example of historical accuracy presented in an exciting, innovative way.

*Collins Dove* **H** 8–12 years ☆

## Fossils Tell Of Long Ago

*Aliki*

An excellent, lively and informative introduction to the topic of fossils which explains how they are formed, and what they tell us. Touches of humour in the illustrations are an added attraction.

*Black* **P** 6–9 years

## The Glorious Flight Across The Channel With Louis Blériot July 25, 1909

*Alice and Martin Provensen*

The Frenchman, Louis Blériot, became obsessed with the desire to fly and after numerous designs, built the Blériot XI which crossed the English Channel in thirty-seven minutes. The thrills, spills and achievements all emerge in the period illustrations.

*Hutchinson* **H** 6–9 years

## Making A Picture Book

*Anne Bower Ingram, illustrated by Bob Graham*

A well-known children's book editor and an illustrator together present the fascinating story behind picture books. Highly effective illustrations include multiple frames, original artwork, roughs and manuscripts from familiar Australian books. Explanations of colour separation and printing processes are particularly clear. Humour throughout wins readers.

*Nelson* **H** 7–10 years ☆

## Mummies Made In Egypt

*Aliki*

People are fascinated with mummies and Aliki reveals all about them in an easy-to-read, clearly illustrated book. The process of mummification is described: the removal of organs, wrapping the body and burial procedures.

*Bodley Head* **H** 7–10 years

## Roland Harvey's Incredible Book Of Almost Everything
*Roland Harvey*
A mind-boggling, whopper-sized, 192-page book of truly 'almost everything'. Games, puzzles, stories, profiles of recording artists, crafts, hints on skiing, throwing frisbees, camping, kite flying, trivia, riddles, informative articles and more, much more.
*Five Mile Press* 🅿
8–12 years ☆

## Children In Australia: An Outline History
*Sue Fabian and Morag Loh*
The changing status of children is examined from pre-European settlement to 1980. An informative text links extensive, provocative quotes and illustrations from primary sources. Topics range from child labour, crime and punishment, education and health to social activities.
*Hyland House* 🅗
10–12 years ☆

## Going West
*Martin Waddell, illustrated by Philippe Dupasquier*
A young girl recounts her family's trip to the American west. Dangers are only briefly referred to but the multiple-frame illustrations show the difficulties. Many aspects of pioneer life in America are detailed and the strengths of various individuals revealed.
*Puffin* 🅿 6–8 years

## The Australopedia
*Joan Grant*
The *Australopedia*'s lively and stimulating style guides the reader through Australian contemporary life and future concerns. Broad sections such as Place, Ourselves and Each Other, Work and Spare Time include fascinating detail with the copious cartoons, graphics and photographs making a visually exciting book for browsing, study, entertainment and information.
*Penguin* 🅗 10 + years ☆

## Burke And Wills
*Roland Harvey*
Robert Burke and William Wills' ill-fated expedition to explore Australia's inland features in picture-book format. Watercolour and line illustrations with fold-outs effectively reveal the isolation, vast distances, searing heat and many disasters.
*Five Mile Press* 🅿 7–10 years ☆

## Your Microwave Cookbook
*Lesley Richardson, illustrated by Daniela Voican*
Microwave cooking is decidedly different from conventional cooking so a book such as this is very helpful for a beginner. Safety tips and details of how a microwave oven works are included — always a plus. The text is clear and interesting and treats the usual food groups with plenty of recipes for daily meals or special occasions.
*Ashton Scholastic* 🅿
9–12 years ☆

## The Great Australian Kid's Almanac
*Stephen Taylor, illustrated by Patrick Cook*
Included are twelve-hundred facts about Australia arranged in alphabetical order. All entries are short, snappy and definitely interesting: disasters, firsts, arts, sport, women, mysteries, food and many other interests are included. Illustrations are humorous and appealing.
*Angus & Robertson* 🅿
7–12 years ☆

## How A Book Is Made
*Aliki*
The production of a book is clearly illustrated in a step-by-step process from the creator's idea to the reader's response. Terminology is clearly defined by illustrations and text. Because the complex process of printing is included as well as the simpler steps, this book is appropriate to a wide age range.
*Scholastic* 🅿 7–10 years

### Science Fun With Mud And Dirt
*Rose Wyler*
Playing in mud turned into enjoyable learning of scientific concepts — it's a winner. Wyler investigates the composition of dirt, describes animals that dig in dirt and presents the interrelationship of plants and soils. Interesting and educational as well.
*Messner* 🄿 6–8 years

### The Secret House
*David Bodanis*
A book which fascinates and repels both children and adults! The author exposes the biological, physical and cultural events of everyday lives using microphotography. No viewer or reader will see the environment in the same way again!
*Simon and Schuster* 🄷 10 + years

### Special Effects
*Rick Clise*
This fascinating glimpse behind the trick effects of the movie trade makes fascinating reading and viewing. Topics covered include monsters, animals, death, fire and optical effects. Movie stills are included of many contemporary and older, memorable movies. Stress is laid on the need for safety precautions and special equipment. Non-readers will devour this one.
*Viking Kestrel* 🄷 9 + years

### A Young Person's Guide To Art In Australia
*Robin Norling (ed)*
Here the reader is introduced to artistic materials and the basic elements of art, such as colour and line. A guide to effective gallery viewing and a range of well-known art works, mostly Australian, are included. Each art work is placed in a social context and includes some details about the artist and occasionally a discussion of the medium used.
*Macmillan* 🄷 9–12 years ☆

### The Aboriginal Children's History Of Australia
Written and illustrated by numerous Aboriginal children around Australia, this book views their own history before and after European settlement. The stories told are frank and subtly demonstrate various influences on this 40,000-year-old culture.
*Rigby* 🄷 7–10 years (Library) ☆

### Family Car Fun Book
*Anne Bower Ingram and Peggy O'Donnell, illustrated by Bob Graham*
Every travelling family with children (or adults young at heart) should have one of these. Games, riddles, jokes, activities for driving to the beach, the desert and the shops, trivia, word and brain teasers and all are offered with Graham's light humorous touch.
*Ellsyd* 🄿 7–10 years (Library) ☆

### Being Born
*Sheila Kitzinger, illustrated by Lennart Nilsson*
Using a simple, poetic text and stunning colour photography, this book traces life from conception to birth. Designed to be used by an adult with a child, the whole process is presented using appropriate terminology a child can understand.
*Grosset & Dunlap* 🄷 6–9 years

### Dinosaurs Walked Here And Other Stories Fossils Tell
*Patricia Lauber*
Scientists' knowledge about dinosaurs has been recently re-examined and new titles such as this one are needed. Excellent colour photographs, reproductions and drawings enhance a crisp, clear and to-the-point text.
*Bradbury* 🄷 9–12 years (Library)

### The Magic School Bus Inside The Earth
*Joanna Cole, illustrated by Bruce Degen*
Ms Frizzle, transports her class to the centre of the Earth. There, through a combined comic strip and narrative format, the class has an incredible lesson in geology. The combined fact and fantastical story is separated for those concerned in a brief author's note. Zany illustrations and humorous escapades add to an irresistible dose of fact.
*Scholastic* 🄿 7–11 years

### Camping
*Anne Ingram and Peggy O'Donnell, illustrated by Bob Graham*
A practical book for children covering all aspects of camping including: campfire tucker, the wilderness code, sleeping gear and some useful knots. Humorous illustrations lighten a sensible and informative text.
*Ellsyd* 🄿 8–12 years ☆

### Furred And Feathered Friends
*Margaret Murrant, illustrated by Rod Scott*
Seventeen Australian native animals feature with brief information on habitats, feeding and breeding habits. Superb illustrations by a wildlife painter are photographic in style and highly informative.
*Lansdowne* 🄷 7–9 years (Library) ☆

### God 'Elp All Of Us
*Meredith Hooper*
Three famous Australian aviators, Ross Smith, Bert Hinkler and Charles Kingsford Smith and their adventurous flights are told of in a simple, interesting style. Maps of the flights and photos of the planes and their pilots add interest. Meredith Hooper's work is of consistently high standard and this is a lively, appealing book.
*Methuen* 🄷 10–12 years

# Children's Book Awards

There are three awards for children's books administered by the Children's Book Council of Australia: the Book of the Year Award: Older Readers; the Book of the Year Award: Younger Readers (formerly Junior Book of the Year); and the Picture Book of the Year Award.

## Book of the Year Awards: Older Readers

1982  *The Valley Between*
Colin Thiele (Rigby)

1983  *Master Of The Grove*
Victor Kelleher (Penguin)

1984  *A Little Fear*
Patricia Wrightson (Hutchinson)

1985  *The True Story Of Lily Stubeck*
James Aldridge (Hyland House)

1986  *The Green Wind*
Thurley Fowler (Lansdowne/Rigby)

1987  *All We Know*
Simon French (Angus & Robertson)

1988  *So Much To Tell You . . .*
John Marsden (Walter McVitty)

## Junior Book of the Year Awards

1982  *Rummage*
Christobel Mattingley, illustrated by Patricia Mullins (Angus & Robertson)

1983  *Thing*
Robin Klein, illustrated by Alison Lester (Oxford University Press)

1984  *Bernice Knows Best*
Max Dann, illustrated by Ann James (Oxford University Press)

1985  *Something Special*
Emily Rodda, illustrated by Noela Young (Angus & Robertson)

## Book of the Year Awards: Younger Readers

1986  *Arkwright*
Mary Steele (Hyland House)

1987  *Pigs Might Fly*
Emily Rodda (Angus & Robertson)

1988  *My Place*
Nadia Wheatley, illustrated by Donna Rawlins (Collins Dove)

## Picture Book of the Year Awards

1982  *Sunshine*
Jan Ormerod (Kestrel)

1983  *Who Sank The Boat?*
Pamela Allen (Nelson)

1984  *Bertie And The Bear*
Pamela Allen (Nelson)

1985  No award

1986  *Felix And Alexander*
Terry Denton (Oxford University Press)

1987  *Kojuro And The Bears*
Junko Morimoto (Collins)

1988  *Crusher Is Coming*
Bob Graham (Lothian)

# Dromkeen Medal winners

The Dromkeen Medal is presented to the person considered to have made the greatest contribution to children's literature in Australia. Anyone can be nominated, not necessarily an author or illustrator.

| | | | |
|---|---|---|---|
| 1982 | Lu Rees | 1985 | Anne Bower Ingram |
| 1983 | Maurice Saxby | 1986 | Albert Ullin |
| 1984 | Patricia Wrightson | 1987 | Joan Phipson |

# Children's Book Clubs and Book Fairs

## Ashton Scholastic Book Clubs

Nothing compares with having your own special bookshelf filled with books you have chosen and bought yourself, and which you can look after and add to over the years. The Ashton Scholastic Book Clubs introduce children to a wide variety of books, with their parents helping them in their choice and encouraging their interests.

There are four Clubs, all designed to meet the needs and interests of children at different stages of their development.

### Wombat Book Club for ages 3 to 5 years

Wombat offers a wide range of hardbacks and paperbacks specially selected to cater for the needs of preschool children. There are also books of interest to parents and teachers of preschool children.

### Lucky Book Club for ages 5 to 8 years

Lucky offers well-illustrated paperbacks for the beginning reader, the developing reader and the independent reader.

### Arrow Book Club for ages 8 to 10 years

Children at this age are at many different levels of abilities and are developing a wide range of interests. Arrow caters for them with a wide variety of books, including stories of all kinds and information books.

### Star Book Club, including Teenage, for ages 10 to 14 years

Star caters for the needs of maturing readers who have established their reading interests. The books selected represent the wide variety available to this age group.

Book Clubs can be operated by a Club secretary chosen from the children themselves, by teachers, or by parents. Separate classes or groups within a school can operate individual Clubs if they desire.

In each state there are Ashton Scholastic Consultants available to help with any aspect of Book Club. Former teachers, they are all willing to visit schools to discuss Book Club with groups of children, teachers or parents. Please contact your State Office for more information. Telephone numbers and addresses are given below:

Ashton Scholastic
PO Box 579
Gosford NSW 2250
Tel: (043) 28 3555
Sydney Metropolitan
Tel: (02) 92 2677

Melbourne
1091 Toorak Road
Hartwell VIC 3124
Tel: (03) 29 3667

Adelaide
254 Halifax Street
Adelaide SA 5000
Tel: (08) 223 7563

Brisbane
Teachers Building
495 Boundary Street
Spring Hill QLD 4000
Tel: (07) 831 8555

Perth
2nd Floor
Teachers Union Building
150 Adelaide Terrace
Perth WA 6000
Tel: (09) 325 1233

ACT
Tel: (062) 54 2064

## Book Fairs

### Great Australian Book Fairs

Children love the Great Australian Book Fairs. They're fun, exciting and stimulate an interest in reading. At the Fairs, children can handle and examine a well-rounded selection of titles and select, buy and take home the book of their choice on the day of the Fair.

Great Australian Book Fairs provide schools with multiple copies of a large range of books covering Grades K-7. The books are displayed for two to three days and sold direct to the children as they visit the Fair.

For more information contact:
Great Australian Book Fairs
Freepost 23
PO Box 525
Gosford NSW 2250

Tel: (008) 02 4840

### Platypus Bill's Book Bazaar

Oldmeadow Booksellers, one of the largest booksellers of children's and educational books in Australia, initiated Platypus Bill's Book Bazaar in 1984. The principal features include high quality books, selected from Australian and overseas publishers, a wide range of titles, a competitive sales commission and a unique option to convert the commission into any books from the wide range of children's books available at Oldmeadow Booksellers.

An information brochure is available from:
Platypus Bill's Book Bazaar
18 Helen Street
West Heidelberg
Victoria 3081
Tel: (03) 459 5377

# Index